RESET

5 Steps to reclaim the life you thought you lost

& learn to love yourself!

Jen Sugermeyer

Recognize,

Eliminate

Structure

Elevate and

Transform your life!

For permission requests, write to the publisher, at jen.sugermeyer@gmail.com.

Visit the author's website at www.jensugermeyer.com

Special thanks to Vickie Gould for exceptional coaching. Photo Credit to Taylor Shea. Book Cover Support Murlin Dale Graham.

ISBN: 978-1-7343066-0-6

Your Journey Guide

PREFACE

My heart stuck to my throat as the plane fought through pockets of air at 35,000 ft above the ground. An invisible iceberg sat on my chest as I gasped to get a breath. I no longer had a cushion sitting under me, the seatbelt across my lap kept me from propelling any higher. "Please, don't let this plane go down, God, I have too much to live for."

A year ago, this was a different story.

My heart palpitated in excitement as the plane fought through pockets of air at 35,000 ft above the ground. I hated my life. I lost who I was, and every day seemed to be another tick mark of failed attempts to get a handle on my life, my thoughts, and my actions. I had no real close friendships, and relationships with men were nothing short of disaster. My mental health was in the garbage, I was miserable in almost all areas of my life. Sure, I would love for this plane to go down, no one would blame me or look down on me for how I died. It would be entirely out of my control.

Scary to think where I was. That was me. The thought of an accidental plane crashing with me in it sounded like a good way to go. I didn't want to live, I didn't know how to. I had given my power over to someone I never invited to set up shop in my soul, and this person was winning the war that raged inside of me. I had no idea who I had become, how I got there, what I stood for, how to be happy, or what I wanted to do with my life.

How could this have been me? I was a corporate woman that seemingly had it put together, but I was bursting at the seams trying everything I could to hold it together. Having two lives was killing me. I was too afraid to let anyone see what was happening inside of me; my thoughts, beliefs, habits, and behaviors would have ruined my career (the only thing I thought was somewhat on a track). Almost everything else felt derailed.

Have you ever looked at yourself in the mirror and wondered who that person was staring back at you? Ever wondered what happened to your path that led you to where you are now? Wondered where that person that had hopes and dreams went? Wondered why everything around you seems out of control? Wondered if you were at a point-of-no-return to find happiness again?

Maybe you promise yourself that every upcoming Monday is going to be a fresh new start. You get optimistic about tomorrow, but tomorrow never seems to come. Moreover, the light at the end of the tunnel has now turned into a freight train coming straight at you and you don't see a way to avoid it.

That is exactly where I was a year ago and I wanted that plane to crash. I had no idea who I had become, or how I had gotten there. I was frustrated because I knew there was more to life, and I was capable of more. I knew I was worth more, and that happiness existed, yet I felt the glass walls around me, I couldn't break the cycle of negative thoughts. I was stuck and I hated where I had landed. I was flat out beat down in defeat. How do I break free? This downward spiral had gone on far too long.

How could this corporate businesswoman, who appeared to have a beautiful life, feel like she had little to no control over it? How could she be so unhappy? How could she hate herself so much? When did I give up my power?

Over a decade, I got stuck in a vortex that kept pulling me lower and lower. When I thought I had reached the bottom, I only found sub-layers to deeper bottoms, and even lower lows. The further I sank, the more disconnected I became with the person I knew I *could* be, and the more isolated I became from the world. The optimism about that fresh new Monday started to wane.

Looking back to where my journey to regain my power began, it seems like eons ago, but it also feels like it was just yesterday. A series of highs and lows, joy and pain, challenges and wins. Albeit the good or the bad, I know I needed things to unfold the way they did, so the new changes in my life would stick. It's easy to want to be at the finish line, but I believe you won't fully grasp what you are doing if you cut corners looking for an easy fix. Had I found a way to fast forward and be where I am today, I would have discovered a temporary band-aid, but I wouldn't have the strength and the tools to stay. It's the process and the journey that keeps me where I am today.

In the past, all too often, this is how my life unfolded...

The alarm went off and no sooner had it began to play had I hit the snooze. There I was, lying on the floor, with my work clothes on from the day before. My head throbbed, breath reeked of alcohol, and apparently, I had passed out after the second bottle of wine. I lay there waiting for the alarm to go off again, and my mind was racing about what happened the evening before. I felt the same crippling fear as I did every morning, trying to remember what I had or had not done the night before, and using breadcrumbs and clues to help piece it together. I made my way up off the floor and into the restroom. There was a woman staring back at me that I didn't recognize. After a long, hot shower, I attempted to rebuild the person on the outside to look presentable and recognizable to the world, but the inside was completely dead. No matter how much makeup I put on my face, and no matter how many lines I filled with foundation, I had no idea who that person was staring back at me. Here, I needed to pull it all together to face the office, my staff, and my superiors, however, every day seemed harder than the last to tie the loose ends of my life together.

From the floor to the office, from the hospital to the office, and from jail to the office- I never knew what my night might behold. How could I? I was a blackout drunk. I could only piece together clues from the evening. When would my luck end where I could no longer run into the office, and my fate end in prison, or worse, when would it end in death? I somehow managed to never miss work, but my life outside the office was nothing short of a train wreck, and I knew the light at the end of the tunnel wasn't my saving grace. It was that train heading straight, towards me.

I felt defeated. Nothing in my life seemed right. I wanted so desperately to be the person I knew I could be, I wanted to let people into my life without fear of what they would see. I wanted to stop being so angry and frustrated all the time. I wanted to progress forward in my life. I wanted my life back. I made the commitment to reclaim my life and I documented my steps along the way. I didn't follow a program. I didn't get a sponsor. I made a commitment to myself, and for the first time, I kept it. I found the keys to give me the life I've always known I was capable of and have helped me gain health, wealth and happiness. Some people may think I should keep this other world of mine a secret forever, but I know that my story will serve you, even if it's not exactly the same as yours. Life piles on all of us and that's what we need to unravel. How you think, how you live, your perception on life can all be changed by the simple steps in this book. If I can break free from where I was, I'm confident you can do the same. I want you to have what I have now and you can.

Before I began this journey, I was contemplating suicide. The thoughts bombarded my mind, and it seemed to be the only way to end the madness. My addiction was not isolated to after-hours, it found a way to take over my brain 24 hours a day, 7 days a week. I was living two lives, and the madness of keeping them separate was getting to be more than I could take. I wanted out, and I didn't know how. The only thing that kept me alive was the thought of ruining Mother's Day, and the fact is that I just wasn't quite ready to end it all, but the thoughts and realness of it all increased daily.

Today, I am not ashamed to allow anyone to peer into my life, and I am not ashamed to share my story. I look in the mirror and I not only know the woman staring back at me, but I truly love and respect her. I am everything I knew I could be and I continue to amaze myself every day at just how beautiful my life is. I took the power back from the person I didn't recognize, created a lifestyle to sustain my new life, and I carry around my box of resources to stay on track.

There are no more excuses- this is my time to shine. This is not like losing weight on a 'fad diet' only to gain it back when I come off it. I want a lifestyle change where I reframe my entire mind and soul so I never get back to where I was at the start of this journey.

I commend you for picking up this book, each one of us needs to be focused on self-care and continual improvement through reflection. The single best thing I've done is to get inside my head, that's when my life started to level out and I found the path to a great life.

We live in a society where people with problems are rarely depicted on TV as the cool girl or guy next door, nor the mom juggling toddlers and a job, or the corporate executive with a successful career. The media glamorizes having it all together and hiding your struggles so that you can show the world someone normal. It perpetuates this need to live in two worlds if you struggle. I'm a proof of that. Life happens to all of us and it can easily get us off track. We lose that connection with the person within and before you know it you are looking in the mirror and not sure how you got there or who is looking back.

It's my mission to help pave the way, break the stigma and create the path for future generations. I hope you will join me. If you had a child, wouldn't you want them to speak up if they were hurting? Instead, they internalize their pain because it was less painful than speaking up for help. Their pain manifests into hopelessness, worthlessness, mental health issues, disease or even death. If only they had said something, then you could have helped, but you didn't know. We need to stop this ideology of shame around speaking up which creates the need to live in two worlds and it starts with you, for you, and for others.

I can't promise you'll get a promotion at work or increase your financial wealth, but I can promise that if you take this seriously and work these steps, you will see a rich impact throughout all areas of your life. I sleep better, my anxiety has reduced significantly, my health and my appearance has improved drastically, and my mental health is no longer in the garbage. I'm able to have deep and personal relationships, and I'm genuinely happy throughout all areas of my life. I no longer live in fear, and I'm at peace. The fruits of the spirit; love, joy, peace, patience, goodness, gentleness are attainable goals and they can be your reality. I took back control over my life and my mind and recognize the face staring back at me in the mirror once again. In fact, I love that face now.

There was a time I would have given anything not live in two worlds, to have my life back from underneath the thumb of addiction. I woke up in fear every day, I had constant anxiety, and my anger was out of control. I hated myself, and I was sick and tired of being sick and tired, without any power over my life. I'm giving you what I would have paid my life savings for in the form of this book.

I am here to support you. I'll be your biggest cheerleader -- let me be that for you in this book. You can do this. If you want your life back on track, if you want to rid yourself of what is weighing you down, if you want to learn to love that person in the mirror then you can have it. It's inside of you. I believe in you.

Every day, I fly a little higher, reaching heights I only dreamed. I knew I could be more, I knew I could do more. I knew I could be happy, but I didn't know how. When I committed myself to change I told myself I was going to give the fight of my life, for my life- this was my last hoorah. As I write this now a tear is tear rolling down my face for the joy and happiness I feel today and the love that I have for myself. Moreover, the sole reason I wrote this book is for you to have it too. If you've been where I've been, you can be where I am.

Buona Lettura!! (Happy Reading!!)

This book is dedicated to my childhood best friend, David Gray, who passed away after he lost the power over his own life. Forever in my heart.

INTRODUCTION:

The Key to Unlocking Everything

Most of us entered kindergarten not worrying if we would pass the class. We went every day and were encouraged to be kind to others, include our classmates, participate in art and singing, and be quiet during nap time. We didn't need to be told to declare what we wanted, we just did. We wore what made us feel great and we happily announced that we were going to be a dinosaur when we grew up, and no one could convince us otherwise.

Then, something happened as we grew up. Somewhere doubt crept in and pretty soon, we lost what we had in kindergarten. At least, that's what happened to me, and I know I'm not alone.

I got overloaded with information, responsibilities, success, failures, and competition. I was told I was different, I was told I wasn't good enough. I got caught in the rat race. I forgot what it was like to be that carefree child that loved to run around with no pants on, not caring about the judgment of the thick thighs and lack of muscle definition. I forgot what it was like to have time to color and how proud I was to show my masterpiece, even if I couldn't color in the lines. I forgot what it was like take a break in the day to rejuvenate my body. I forgot what it's like to have a best friend and the joy from the childish banter during playtime.

I grew up.

Just like so many of us did.

I lost myself striving for this thing called perfection, and I was caught in the fast lane of life without slowing down to see where I was. Many of us wake up one day and we don't know how we got to where we are, but we're here, and we're miserable.

That was me. I had sped through life and I have little recall of the journey. It was fast, it was hard, it was confusing, it was lonely, and it was competitive. Now, I stand here naked, and

I'm not seeing what I saw when I was 5. I see a monster inside of me of who I've become, and I loathe how I look on the outside. I don't identify with the person I am today, but congratulations, Jen, you're a successful woman in corporate America - you've arrived. And yet, I still had a huge fear that my secret world would collide with my public world and I would lose everything I had.

I got so busy with life that I forgot who I was. Maybe it's the same with you. Good news is that it's not hard to get back there and get back to the basics. All you have to do is commit to you, get honest, self-reflect and make those small changes in your life. We can get YOU back to loving the person you see in the mirror!

Inside this book, I have detailed my trademarked methodology, 'RESET,' that I developed while resetting my own life, so I could get my life back. The five steps to RESET include: Recognize, Eliminate, Structure, Elevate, and Transform.

Along the way, I have included questions to answer, and exercises to complete to make sure you have an understanding of how to best implement these ideas in your own life. You've got this!

Disclaimer: This book provides general information and discussions about health and related subjects. The information and other content provided in this book, or in any linked materials, are not intended and should not be construed as medical advice, nor is the information a substitute for professional medical expertise or treatment.

If you or any other person has a medical concern, you should consult with your health care provider or seek other professional medical treatment. Never disregard professional medical advice or delay in seeking it because of something that you have read in this book or in any linked materials. If you think you may have a medical emergency, call your doctor or emergency services immediately.

PART 1- **A Hard Reset Overview - Reclaiming my Life**

My breath felt infused with lidocaine. I never felt. I preferred the tingling sensation rather than dealing with life. Feeling meant I had to face reality, which I had successfully run from for decades. I didn't want to face who I was, what I had done, and what was done to me. At this point, my addiction wanted me to drink, and that's what I did. I felt no pain. No pain at least when I was drinking, it was every other hour of the day that I was miserable, but at least at 5pm, my life would be manageable. I loathed feelings, so I buried them inside, and they were buried deep. I created an unmanageable life in order to feel it was manageable and I ran this hamster wheel for decades. I was a walking zombie through this thing called life- I felt like the living dead. What a life.

I hated that person. I didn't identify with her, yet she was stronger than I was. She made me believe I needed her, and that I needed the life she created, that I needed to hide away from the world because of the shame I endured. That wench -- when did she get invited to the party?

There was a humbling aura in the room as we both sat down to have 'the talk'. The relationship needed work and, as opposed to previous relationships, we sat as two adults willing to open up and communicate about what needed to be improved to keep the relationship alive.

I shied away from relationships for years in fear of what might be seen, what I tried so desperately to hide might be uncovered. There I was, sitting in front of a man I thought would be the solution to my problem, the ingredient to my life that make me want to stop drinking and help me find true happiness, and here we were discussing why our half-baked relationship was not moving forward. I was about 99% confident what his assessment would be. He had to know I was an alcoholic, as much as I tried to hide. My teeth grinded together as he started to speak. I was bracing for a scolding of what I already knew and utterly despised about myself. I wanted no one to know about this other life in me that existed and that consumed my thoughts -- this life that I tried to hide, the life that was going to take the better half of me if I didn't get a hold of it. There we sat, I was ready to be reprimanded.

As my internal army stood guard at the top of the wall I had built, he uttered seven unforgettable words, "Jen, you need to learn to love yourself."

I stared back at the face of a man I had dated for a mere 4 months and for once I was speechless. A summary of my life seemed to race through my mind: what I had done, where I was, and most importantly, I saw a future that was entire empty and alone. He was right. I didn't love myself. I could not dispute that statement. I was broken, at best, and there was nothing the army at the top of my wall could do to help protect me from his words. I cracked wide open in that moment.

I had a lot of rock bottoms. When I didn't think I could go any lower, I always managed to find a way. I knew I could not openly discuss my life, there was too much stigma around not having a 'picture of perfect' life. How could a successful and confident woman in the corporate world be an alcoholic? How could she end up in jail? How could she end up hospitalized because of her addictions? How could she wind up in a physically and verbally abusive relationship where she would have to blame her black eyes and bruises on boxing to her coworkers? How could a woman to whom others looked up to suffer so deeply and yet continue to do well at work, climb the corporate ladder, have a group of intelligent and supportive friends, be a tax-payer, a church goer, and appear to have it all together?

It's simple -- poor mental health doesn't discriminate. Issues don't target races. Pain isn't isolated to certain income levels. Struggles don't happen to "those other people". Anything can happen to anyone. But, society has created a misnomer that people who struggle look a certain way and we've created a stigma that keeps people and their struggles in hiding. We have a culture where it's frowned upon to raise your hand and say the words, 'mental health' and God-forbid make it known we need help. I was a businesswoman and yet my mental health was in the trash. I was too afraid to speak up for fear of losing my job. I was afraid of tarnishing my reputation, I was afraid of ruining my career. So, I hid what I didn't want to be seen. I hid what I knew society would frown on. I hid what the world perceived as weak. My inability to have one life that I could share with others held me back across all areas of my life, including the ability to have a meaningful and healthy relationship.

There I sat, all of those fears flooding my brain, and I knew I could no longer hide. I was unable to live a life I wanted. I knew I despised where I was in my addictions and my mental health, but I pretended they didn't really exist by keeping them hidden. But, they did exist and this double life was slowly killing me and it stole my joy. I didn't want to be alone, but I couldn't keep lying to myself or any potential partner.

I don't know how long I sat there in silence, but it felt like time froze for what seemed like 20 minutes while my mind raced through my dark past, my stark reality, and the hopeless feeling for tomorrow. He didn't tell me anything I didn't already know. I knew I hated the person I had become. I was used to being scolded or punished for my actions (some people did get a small glimpse of my reality at times), but never had anyone come at me with care and concern in such a humble and meaningful manner. I don't believe he knew the full extent of my problems, but he knew enough to know there was more than what met the eye.

It was time. For over a decade, I had failed attempts of claiming power over my life while trying to solve a symptom and not the problem. Now, this was it. I was no longer going to be a victim and pretend my issues didn't exist, I was no longer going to wait for Monday to start over. I was no longer going to feed the demon. I wanted my life back and I was going to do whatever it took to get there.

I looked at his brown eyes staring back at me, wondering what he might have thought as my mind wandered the universe. My lips found their senses and I finally uttered, "I'm committing to you, to us, and more so, to me that I *will* learn to love myself. You have my word."

It was such a simple statement, but the most profound one that anyone had ever said to me. I don't believe this man knew what impact this small statement would have on me -- it was probably no more than an innocent observation. There was no way he knew the depth and breadth of my battles. He was, however, close enough to me to see the absence of self-love in all areas I tried so hard to cover up and hide. Seven simple words that cracked me wide open. I was ready to be scolded, I was ready to be shamed, but I was not prepared to have my emotions tapped into and thrown on the table. I knew this was far more than stopping a behavior. I was going to have to face every emotion, every feeling, and every situation I had tried so deeply to ignore and suppressed, and I would come face-to-face with the person that I loathed. If I wanted true happiness, this was the only way. I needed to address the true problem at hand. He saw through to my soul and he knew I was living a lie. I was not as confident as I portrayed. I was a coward. I was lost and I was in a lot of pain. I failed for over a decade. Every day I tried to break free, but every day, I found myself with a bottle. It was time to hit RESET.

Not in my wildest dreams would I have imagined I would be where I am today. Sure, I wanted to be happy and I cried about wanting happiness. I was jealous of others that were happy, but I don't think I ever imagined how it would actually feel and what it would look like. I don't know that, through the tears and dismay I felt about my life, did I have any real idea of what I was desiring. I just knew that my life was not what I wanted, and I was convinced there was more.

I would see people that were happy, and their happiness and success would shape my definition of how my own happiness and success should look. I would see a happy family and think to myself that I would be happy if I was married with kids. I would see a wealthy person and think I would be happy if I was wealthier. I would see someone that had, in my mind, a perfect body, and think I would be happy if I also had a perfect body. I would see someone that was successful in their career, and I would think that I would be happy if I had a certain job title. I looked at the external pieces of everyone's life, and those became definitions of success and happiness.

What I failed to look at was the other side of every equation. Not everyone that is in a marriage is happy, not everyone with kids is happy, not everyone with a perfect body is happy, and not everyone that is wealthy is happy. I looked at the external definitions of happiness and never looked below the surface to realize that none of those things actually guaranteed happiness-- it all comes from within.

When this gentleman called me out and told me I needed to learn to love myself, it was like salt on open wounds. I could never have predicted my journey or the outcome, but that salt launched me into the greatest journey of my life. I discovered I had found the key that unlocked everything that I will walk you through inside this book.

You see, I knew I needed a change, I just didn't know from what and I didn't know how. But, I had committed to myself and I was bound and determined to figure it out. Turns out, I had been going after the wrong problem all along and it was time to face myself head on.

Maybe you feel this way too, maybe you know you also need a change. You're not sure what, but you know you are not where you want to be and you don't have the level of happiness you know you deserve. Maybe you've experienced happiness before and you know you're no longer there or maybe you have never experienced true happiness, but you believe in your core that it's possible. Knowing where I am in my life now, I can truly say that I never had experienced the level of happiness that I have today. Yes, there were times I can say were fun and I enjoyed myself, but there was always something missing.

My symptoms started a long time ago. When I was 12, I started down a dangerous road of self-hate. I was told I was too tall, I was told I was fat and I believe them. I didn't see this person when I was my 5-year-old self full of self-love, I learned to hate myself. I learned to look down on myself and I believed what they said. The layers in life can start young, those layers that we pile on ourselves that disconnect us from the person within.

I didn't have high self-esteem before my eating disorder started and my thoughts about myself only spiraled once I started to harm and shame my body. It was here I learned the mastery of living a double life. Two worlds became the norm, I didn't know any different. I was the person you saw in front of you, but there was also a dark and evil side that I kept hidden. One addiction led to another and all of a sudden, I was in my mid-thirties a full blown alcoholic that spent her nights chain smoking cigarettes and drinking until she passed out.

I truly believed there was more in life for me. I knew that

waking up on the floor of my apartment in my work clothes on a Tuesday in my mid-thirties, was not the life I was destined to live. I didn't know how to escape. I didn't know how to get my life on a track that I felt proud about. I didn't want anyone to get too close to me for fear of what they may see, and yet I yearned for close friends and a relationship in my life.

I despised the face looking back at me in the mirror. I never openly invited her in to take residence but she did. The person I tried to hide from the world could not hide from the shame I faced in the mirror even if I was the only one that could see it.

I finally had enough, I knew I was at a crossroad in my life. I was going to end up in prison or dead if I didn't make a change; neither fate would I have imagined for myself as I think of that vivacious, young girl chasing fireflies. It was on that day when he said that I needed to learn to love myself that I said enough-is-enough and I committed to turning my life around. I had to stop making excuses and face everything head-on. No more. It was time to take back my life, my actions, my mind, my today, and my tomorrow.

During this time, I made an important discovery that I believe is the crux to the path to success: self-reflecting and being honest with ourselves is the only way to achieve the results you are looking for. We can get so twisted up in life and before we know it we have these layers and piles on top of the person we know is within, and yet we haven't stopped along the way to self-reflect and get honest about where we are. We don't ask how we feel. We don't bother to check in and make sure that we are doing ok in the midst of it all. That's how we get disconnected with ourselves-- life takes us by storm and we get swept away to a place we didn't expect to be.

The thing is, you don't have control over anything except yourself, so we need to learn to challenge ourselves and take ownership of our minds. It's only when you stop romanticizing about what you're doing and what's happening in your life that you can completely commit to making that change. You are the only captain of your ship, and not for just today, but for your entire life. My last Day 1 was different because I was ready, I was defeated, I was broken. I knew I needed to self-reflect and finally get honest with that woman in the mirror that I didn't recognize-- my future depended on it.

It boils down to a choice for you too. You can continue to be your own worst enemy, or you can learn to be your biggest advocate. I'll tell you this, my life is 1000% better when I committed to me. It's a choice you make, it's entirely up to you on how you want your life to go. It's no magic formula that only a few lucky people are fortunate to experience, it's the simple steps in this book that will take you to a level of happiness and peace that you own and control.

Let me walk you through my journey at a high-level so you can see just how this works, then we'll dig into the details in Part 2 on how to actually implement these steps. I want you to see the flow that happened in my life, how easy it can be, then we'll get you there by the end of this book. This methodology is a holistic approach to revamping your life. It doesn't address just one area or one problem, but rather looks at the composition of your landscape and puts your life in harmony. You may have one issue to address or many, and this methodology is designed to bring you structure, clarity and the mindset to keep you dialed in to happiness. Whatever isn't serving you will fall off in this process. Trust the process, it's a proven method that I can personally attest to. The five steps in RESET include:

Recognize- Recognizing and committing to change. No more excuses, no more playing victim, you take full ownership and accountability for your life.

Eliminate- Eliminate what doesn't serve you in your life. People, places, things and ideologies. Anger, negativity, self-hate is eliminated in this step.

Structure- You develop a plan to keep out what you've determined does not serve you. You determine your standards and boundaries and keep out what will hold you back.

Elevate- You elevate your life by living in your purpose, by living in the moment and finding gratitude in all you have and don't have.

Transform- You structure your life so you can have a lifestyle that supports the life you want to have. A life where you keep power over your mind and your life. It's the check and balance when things start to veer off track.

Here was my journey.

~~~~

I was knocking on deaths' door playing Russian Roulette with my life, it was only a matter of time until something went sideways that I couldn't recover from. I had tried in the past to make changes, but I was never truly at a point where I was ready so I never took my progress seriously. Whenever I would get any amount of sobriety, even a day, I always missed the addiction. I always wanted its comfort and I was jealous of others who could partake in drinking when I would not. But this time I had hit that space of hollowness because I thought I was entirely alone in the world. The one thing that comforted me in my time of need was not only holding me back, it was slowly killing me before everyone's eyes. This was a do or die for me, and I knew there was more for me other than ending up 6-feet under.

RECOGNIZE

I was sick and tired of being sick and tired, and I didn't want to end up being another statistic lost to poor mental health. I was committed to going down a path to remove those strongholds from my body once and for all. I wanted a healthy mind, I wanted a healthy life. It was a battle that had already almost taken my life on many numbers of occasions. If I wanted real change, I had to make some real changes. Every person, place, thing, and ideology needed to be assessed. I was committed to change at whatever cost.

I realized what was different this time was that my desire to stop my destructive behaviors was stronger than my desire to have them in my life. Where I used to take comfort in that bottle was no longer comfortable. Moreover, where that secret world used to be my safe space is now thought of as dangerous. I flipped the switch in my mind and turned those two worlds around.

I knew I had to get honest with myself. If I continued to lie to myself and pretend the issue didn't exist then I was going to keep failing. I didn't need to go profess everything to the world, but I had to get honest with myself.

Excuses were out. I was no longer going to entertain any excuses and finally take the ownership in my life. I was done. No more blaming traffic, no more saying I don't have time, no more blaming anyone else- the excuses were no longer going to be acceptable in my life. This also played into the victim mentality.

I used to think, "Why me?" far too often. Why was I the one in my family that had to end up with addiction? Why was I the one that had to go through a divorce by the time I was 30? Why was I the one that had to carry such a heavy load on my back day-in and day-out? Why was I not as well off as the rest of my family? Why was I blessed with the challenge of finding large shoes, extra long pants, and all of the thousands and thousands of height comments I would get throughout my life? Now, these are all blessings that I don't question why anymore. I stopped questioning and started accepting (and even liking) them. I tell people that I don't have any regrets or ill feelings in life, but instead I have a lot of rich lessons, and this was a mind shift I had to make.

No more 'poor me', no more feeling sorry for myself, no more blaming others for my life. I had to take accountability for my mind, my life and own it. If I wanted to be a success story then I needed to stop the finger pointing, stop the excuses, stop placing blame on everything else and take true ownership of my life.

I also knew that I was exhausted doing this on my own. I wanted a higher power, someone more omnipotent than myself to guide me and take the weight of the world off my shoulders. I was beat down and I knew that through the course of my life that when I was closer to my higher power that my life was better than doing it solo. It was time to jump into the passenger seat and relinquish that control over my life. I had already driven it into the ground, I had proven to be unsuccessful on my own. Learning to give over this level of control was not only part of my success, but it was a huge weight that came off my shoulders. I was finally given a level of comfort and peace knowing I was being watched over and provided for, which was a feeling I yearned for, yet I never knew it.

The last big concept to grasp as part of the recognizing process was allowing myself to be vulnerable. I knew vulnerability would need to be part of my journey. I had covered up my entire life, even to myself, and uncovering was surely going to bring an element of pain, but I had to allow myself to be exposed to this risk. I also knew that in order to feel love, joy, peace, kindness, courage, empathy, and every other feeling that I had lost touch with, I would have to be vulnerable. It's the core to all feelings. Without taking the risk of being happy, I would never know what happiness was. I had masked my feelings for so long, and in order to sort them out and address them, I had to be willing to open up and face them head on. By exposing myself, this meant I would have to deal with the hurt, the repercussions, rejection, the love, the acceptance, and everything that would result from opening up. Furthermore, I had to be able to accept the outcome. No more playing numb. By opening up, I would be able to fully dig into my life, expose and address each area.

I knew this meant I was going to need to admit things, do things, and address things that were going to make me feel uncomfortable or bad about myself. I was committed to change by saying enough-is-enough, eliminating excuses, cleaning up my immediate surroundings and allowing myself to be vulnerable to set the foundation for me to start the work in my mind.

These are all conceptual, but they're fundamental. If you are ready to make change then you need to get out of your own way and make it happen. Recognizing is acknowledging and committing to yourself and laying the basic ground rules for your mindset.

ELIMINATE

Now we start to get into the fun.

After committing to change, the first thing I did was take a hard assessment of my surroundings and what was distracting me or blocking me from connecting with myself. This also cleared the way for living in gratitude, finding my purpose and other concepts we'll get into further on into the methodology. If there is something weighing you down, blocking you from your goals or distracting you then it's going to be harder if not impossible to meet your goals. I was creating a space I wanted to be in, not vacate to that "other Jen." What could I change in order to make me love this life and create a better breeding ground that was conducive for change? Anything that unnecessarily cluttered my space or was toxic to my life needed to go. This was people, places, things and ideologies.

I went through my home and donated anything that did not serve me a purpose. If I had something in my home that I had mild to neutral feelings towards (I didn't love it and I didn't hate it), it was gone. If there was something that did not make me feel good, or if it had negative vibes, it was gone. If there was ANYTHING that had a bad memory, it was gone. I didn't care if an item still had a tag on it or was recently purchased. If there was a bad memory or something was not serving a purpose then I wanted it out of my home.

1. Clean out
2. Donate
3. Liberate
4. Done

Imagine sitting in a mud pit and trying to clean yourself off. You keep pouring water on yourself, but the mud just seems to dilute, not go away. It is the same concept as if you are trying to clean up your life and you are surrounded by things and people that drag you down, distract you, or don't add value to you. You're just being weighed down when you are trying to rise above! There is a kind of force that wants to keep pulling you down much like gravity, but when we eliminate negativity like those things I got rid of, then we actually start to rise.

My material possessions were relatively quick to go through, but now, I also needed to assess the people in my life that were negative. Some people I had to keep at bay, some people I had to remove entirely. These were the people that were going to hold me back from reaching my potential.

After I stripped out the people dragging down my soul, as well as the meaningless or bad memory items from my surroundings, it was then that I had a clearer picture of my life. I wasn't surrounded by distractions. I was able to see exactly what I found meaningful and purposeful. It's like a sieve. It will filter out the unwanted and leave behind the desirable purposeful items.

Removing those unnecessary and damaging people, places and things in my life helped me to not only create a more uplifting environment around me, but also to be able to visualize better what was truly important to me by removing the distractions. In a sense, it was kind of like moving in to a model home; there was furniture, a few nice decorations on the wall, and a pool in the backyard. It was up to me to now personalize and make this model home *MY* home, my new world.

Oh, but the anger I carried. I acknowledge I held a great deal of anger because it was proved by my actions. I don't think I realized just how much anger I was harboring until I reflected on the far too many times I did get angry. I felt like I was a yo-yo bouncing from happy thoughts to angry thoughts all day long. I was not cognizant of this behavior at first, but I realized it gave me a high level of anxiety, and I came to understand that I needed to work on removing it if I wanted to heal and be healthy.

My autopilot response in far too many situations was to get angry, annoyed, and anxious or upset. I was a ticking-time-bomb. I hated how out of control I would get when I was driving. I would say and do things that I would never do to someone's face. I allowed myself to get ragingly mad. I would curse, flip people off, and use my big vehicle to 'teach people a lesson' if they 'needed to be taught a lesson'. Just looking at those words written down makes me sick to my stomach. I was this way almost every time I was in a vehicle-- what a drastic change from where I am today. I thought I was keeping the anger isolated and unseen from the people around me (just another part of my double life), but it just kept me from getting close to people in the end.

It was one thing to diffuse the situation and stop myself from getting angry, but letting go was an entirely separate element that I needed to master. I had to catch myself before the anger would spiral out of control and rewire the situation in my brain by telling myself that it wasn't worth the anxiety and strain on my life. I had to learn to focus only on those things I could control. I had to learn to give it over to my higher power to work the situation-- it wasn't mine to own.

I actively sought to replace negative situations with positive ones. It was like creating a story for every situation I came across. I would make up a reason for why someone was a bad driver, why someone had to stop on a moving walkway, why someone had no common sense that day! Whatever the situation was, and as funny as it may sound, I had to force myself to turn these situations around in my mind until it became natural. As humans, we often seek justification in our minds, a reason for a behavior. I created situations in my mind that justified their behavior (entirely made up), which then helped me to stop controlling the situation in my mind and make me more positive. Additionally, focusing on being more positive helped me to let go of things. Think about how many times you let someone get under your skin for doing something nice. No, that doesn't happen. Things fester when you are angry or annoyed, so I had to remove those elements and it helped to allow me to let go of the situation in my mind, and made me a more positive person overall.

I began to surround myself with people that emitted the energy that I wanted in my life. We all have an energy we emit and it can fluctuate throughout the day. You've probably met that person that just exudes joy, happiness, peace, love or confidence. Their energy is infectious. You love the feeling you get when you are around that person and it makes you feel warm and happy when you get around the energy. That is the energy you want to strive to have in your life; positive, uplifting, enriching. We want to attract that energy in our close circle, and we do so by becoming the person we want to attract.

It wasn't that I entirely gave up people in my life that didn't have the energy I wanted around me (some are impossible to avoid), but I started to look at where everyone fit and how much I wanted to be around them. I could see that the more positivity I was around, the more positive I felt because like attracts like. I started to observe the negativity around me and it was repelling. It polarized with the new positive energy coming from within me. It's like oil and water-- they just don't mix.

Lastly, I had to learn the concept of letting go. There was so much in my past and in my life that I held on to. I was not able to move forward because shackles held me back. I had to learn to forgive and let go, and in doing so I was able to move ahead in my life without resentment and unnecessary baggage.

STRUCTURE

You've now eliminated what doesn't belong and now you need to structure your life to keep you operating within a space of peace, happiness and power.

I needed to learn to love myself and to start appreciating and loving myself for who I was at that moment, in spite of imperfections and all. No more hiding. That was the single statement that catapulted me into the change I needed after all. Since I didn't fully understand what all this entailed, I started with the only thing that made sense. I did what I could to make it a point to externally remind myself, and so, I created post-it notes and put them on my mirror.

- You are beautiful
- You are worth it
- You are a good friend
- You are worth someone's time
- You are a daughter
- You are a sister
- Your smile lights up a room

See, any repeated activity becomes habitual, so I redirected my thought patterns and stopped the self-hate messages I told myself for so long. I replaced them with positive and supportive messages. If you tell yourself that you are not able to do something, then you won't be able to. If you tell yourself you're worthless, then you'll believe you're worthless. If you tell yourself that you aren't enough, then you'll believe you aren't enough. Therefore, I reframed the way my mind was thinking, and told myself the opposite of everything I had been telling myself for decades.

I listened to self-help recordings as I went to sleep. I looked in the mirror and forced myself to say that I was worth it. After some time, I started to believe that I was enough, was beautiful, and was worth it. Low and behold, I started to like myself too. This was how I started to change from being my worst enemy to my biggest advocate. I had a completely new perspective about myself.

It was shocking to realize how much our minds control everything; our thoughts, actions, perception, our reality, and the outcome. My brain needed to stop running loose and focus in the right areas, and not every dark nook and crevice it could find. As I turned the ship's bow, I finally started to give my life the boundaries it needed, so I could live a healthy life.

Standards and boundaries are more than not having sex on

the first date. Boundaries dictate how you operate in every situation. Upon assessing my life, I saw that I had allowed so much gunk to creep in because I had not appropriately formalized my position on different situations. I'm talking about my stance on the negativity I would allow in my space, the amount of time I would dedicate to work, the amount of time I would dedicate to self-reflection and self-love, the people in my life, my bedtime, and how I would allow myself to be treated. It was everything!

We all have some level of standards we have established in our lives as I'm sure you would say we have a moral compass and try to follow it. Sure, I was not out committing crimes and being a deviant to society. I'm not talking about that kind of standard. I'm talking about the guidelines you have given yourself (our governance) for our daily lives. This is our playbook, it's how we respond when the offense makes a move. I was playing a game of life without a playbook so I was coming up with a new defensive strategy every time the offense made a new move!

After setting standards and boundaries, made the decision that just like getting rid of physical things in my house, I was only going to spend my time focused on purposeful activities. Sometimes, the purpose was that my body needed rest and some well-deserved time on the couch was my activity, and I was okay with that. Whatever it was, if it served me and my needs (joy being one of those needs), then I was willing to spend the time. Otherwise, if it didn't then I was not willing to invest my precious time that had been so graciously given back to me (this excludes mandatory obligations we have in life). These were boundaries I set for myself and they helped me to focus on what would improve my life and keep it on track.

One important boundary I needed to implement was standing up for myself. Maybe it was for lack of wanting confrontation or the fact that I was concerned with the repercussions of speaking up for myself, but I lacked in this area. At work, I had no problem standing up for what I believed to be true. But, as I noted in past relationships, I allowed guys to put other priorities above me, and I accepted that behavior (I was frustrated by it, but had I set the boundary in place then I would have avoided feeling neglected). It was in these passive areas, where I needed to enhance my communication outwardly. I was allowing myself to get 'run over', which in turn would make me feel worse about myself.

I used to have very strong feelings against asking anyone for a helping hand, but I actually found this was a critical piece to the puzzle. There is an intrinsic element of relationship where there is an ebb and flow. This flow needs to happen between individuals-- it's a give and take. Think about how draining it would be to have a friend that was always asking for support but was unwilling to offer a hand. At some point, this would get old and the relationship would probably fizzle away. My friends would often ask how they could help and I would politely say no. As a friend, it's in their nature to want to help, and by my rejecting their help, I was not allowing the flow of friendship to happen. Instead, I was not allowing the relationship to reach its potential. I was blocking part of the essentials of a friendship.

Lastly, I acknowledged and accepted that I simply could not do everything on my own. When I committed to making changes in my life I went through a lot of changes and there were times I sincerely needed some help. I had to stop being so stubborn and had to humble myself and simply just ask. It really was not as intimidating as it seemed, but it was something I had to force myself to do. I remember sending my friend a text asking for some help around the house. I found myself saying "I hate asking," and, "It's ok to say no," and, "I don't want to send this message, but I'm going to hit 'send' real quickly before I change my mind." Silly, actually. My friends would always respond with, "Of course! I'd be happy to!" I made myself anxious and uncomfortable for what? My friends said they were more than happy to help because that's what friends are for.

Asking for help is not only an essential piece to a true friendship, but I had to face the reality that I simply could not do everything on my own (nor do I really want to). Candidly, it was really nice not to have to YouTube everything and try to figure it out on my own. I just had to get out of my own way and stop being so stubborn.

ELEVATE

Living in an elevated state requires some understanding and focus, but the ground work from eliminating and structuring have paved the way to make this undoubtedly an enjoyable step in the process. It's about elevating your life and finding your happiness.

I focused on filling my life with people, places and things that I felt would bring meaning and purpose. Since I had cleared out the clutter, I could now focus on what truly brought me joy and add things that gave me purpose. I began volunteering, I committed to joining a church and being an active participant. I made time for me and took care of myself. I built downtime into my schedule, and I started to fill my life with things that gave me a purpose and made me feel good.

A natural change started to happen in my life in this stage. As a result of being more positive and minimizing my life, I started to truly understand the concept of gratitude. I started to be thankful for what was in my life that I had never noticed before. I stopped overlooking things. I used to wake up every morning and wish I was still sleeping, or wish I could stay in bed, or I would hit the ground running and go for a workout. Now, I'm so grateful I've been given another day to live. I took many of the basics in life as if they were promises (and was even annoyed and angry with some of them), and yet nothing is a guarantee. Your limbs, your life, your family, your house, your mode of transportation, your job, and your pet -- nothing is guaranteed. It's a bit humbling to think that everything we have is not in our full control and can be taken away. Even the hard lessons in life and the purpose they served are things to be grateful for.

Every little thing in my life has become a lesson, a blessing, a gift, a course correction, or an honor. I accept what happens and I do not dwell on the situation. If it's a lesson, learn from it. If it's a gift, embrace it. If it's a course correction, shift lanes. If it's an honor, take it with a smile. Finding peace with your higher power and a heart of gratitude will help shift what you do and what happens in life to a positive mindset.

Learning gratitude was truly a mind shift, and today, I can even find gratitude in the abusive relationship I was in. Having been with a narcissistic and physically abusive man, I now have compassion, empathy and strength to help others. I understand what it's like to be the focus of attention in the beginning of a relationship, to feel beautiful and doted upon, only to quickly shift to being the pawn used to elevate an ego. I understand what it's like to have your perception of reality manipulated so you can see through the lens he wants you to see through. I understand what it's like to be told that you are always wrong, and yet you're led to believe that you need the relationship and can't function without it. I understand the mental anguish of not feeling like you're ever enough, and always going the extra mile to make the other person happy even if that means fueling your addiction when you don't want to. I understand how it feels to cry yourself to sleep night after night, wondering why you can't do anything right, and the worthless feeling you get when you're belittled and manipulated.

That hell made me stronger. Had I not gone through what I went through, I may not have the level of strength and courage I have today, and I know what boundaries I need to set in my life to avoid this going forward. I now acknowledge I need to prioritize myself in my life as my own number one. Although the circumstances were grim, I am grateful for how it ultimately strengthened me. It helped me to identify comparable characteristics that throw up red flags. It gave me a better appreciation of what a relationship should not look like. For the relationship ending when it did-- for that, I am truly grateful.

TRANSFORMATION

Once I grasped these concepts that we just reviewed at a high level then I needed to make my transformation permanent. I needed to learn the tools to keep what I had learned in check. I didn't want to do something once, see benefit and then forget. Just like a commitment to the gym— if I wanted to lose weight then it was going to need to be a lifestyle I adopted. The last part of the methodology was the transformation and how to stay on track.

~~~~

Moreover, through all these various steps I discovered the key to unlocking everything. As I reflected on my 1-year journey I set out on, not only had I learned to love myself, but also, doors were opening, and my life was changing. I was able to sleep better. I felt at peace and I felt closer to my job (not because I was working more, but because I was grateful for the purpose it served in my life). I was being recognized at work, and I was able to drive to work without any anger. My finances started to align. I was able to open up and share my life with others, which ultimately brought us closer. I was able to give more to others. I was able to help people and give advice, and best of all, I was able to look in the mirror and recognize who I was, and I loved the person staring back at me. For the first time, my heart felt ready to finally share with someone.

I am not just excited for the future, but I'm excited for today. I'm eager to see what each day has in store for me, and what I can give back in return. I believe that my life and my scars were a gift. Whereas I once saw them as a culmination of failures, I now know my scars strengthened me into the person I am today, and they gave me the wings to fly. All of the pain was actually building my character and helping to give me a deeper and richer perspective of the world. For all those lessons, I am truly grateful. They have given me a story that not only built me, but one I can now share with you to help you through your trials. Whereas I believe I was once defined by my past, I realized that not only was this false, but that our past serves us merely as building blocks to bring us where we are today.

Wherever you are in your life, if you're looking at someone in the mirror that you no longer recognize, or you know that you need a change-- if you've lost power over an area or all areas of your life, isn't it time to take your life back? Do a RESET! You are worth it! I realized there was a connection of mind, body and soul that needed to be in sync to truly get to know who I was, and to really get to understand and love me as a person. Finally, I broke that cycle of addiction, I smashed behaviors that were holding me down, I got my mental health back from the gutter and claimed power over my life in the process.

Whatever that black cloud is for you that doesn't seem to go away-- change can happen. You can create one world you love to be in. Claim victory over your mind, build your future, use those scars as your building blocks, and get the health, wealth, love and happiness in your life. It's five easy steps and those steps will take you to the life you desire, the life you deserve and achieve the results you want.

PART 2- Time to RESET

Think about building your life like building a house. You have to start with the foundation and build up. If you try to build the top floor before you have a solid bottom floor, then you will not have the support needed to hold up the top. The building will be crooked, sink down on one side, and potentially develop cracks. The same is true when you are working your way through this book. If you try to do it all at once, then you run the risk of missing a foundational element. When beginning the book, try to isolate topics and work on them until you fully grasp the concept. Once you are in motion and understanding the changes happening inside you, then you can do them in parallel. You'll find they all overlap and are interwoven at the finish line.

I would suggest taking and working each chapter for at least a week before you start to move to the next, and don't rush if you need more time. It's only to your benefit if you truly conceptualize and understand the transformation that is happening. I want you to achieve the results you are looking for so be realistic with yourself in the speed to which you start to really work the steps.

Remember that game when you were a kid where you would sit in a circle and you'd start with one word, then the next person would build onto your word, and so on and so forth, until a complete sentence had been built? This is how you need to embark on this journey-- one step at a time.

There were times life seemed daunting by everything I 'needed' to do that without fail, I would get overwhelmed, and I would revert to the same destructive behavior I was trying to eliminate. It was easy to run to the old rather than deal with the new. You see for years, I didn't take time to really assess what I was working through and anchor in the new things in my life. I wasn't able to feel and analyze where I was at each stage. All I could think of was:

I need to:

- Eat right
- Cut back on sugar
- Get enough sleep
- Exercise
- Volunteer
- Go to church
- Pray
- Call my parents
- Be social
- Be a good friend
- Do something nice for me
- Go to work
- Pay my bills
- Keep my truck clean
- Clean my sheets every two weeks
- Wash my towels every week
- Fold my laundry
- Put the dishes away
- Go to the dentist 1x year
- Get a physical 1x year
- Go to my lady doc 1x year
- Get blood work done to make sure I'm healthy
- Get my eyes checked annually
- Donate to good causes
- Keep up with my friends
- Make sure there is cat food and clean liter box

Life! So many rules! Information overload would shut me down every time. I would get overwhelmed and lose sight of what I was trying to accomplish. Without fail, 100% of the time, I reverted to my old life and my old way of thinking having made no progress in my life other than acknowledging I wanted more out of my life. I ended up right where I started-- annoyed with myself and reprimanding my lack of follow through.

So, what do you need to do?

First:

Work this program slowly, give it the time it needs to sink in and make sense. I saw some progress immediately. After 6 months, I noticed a difference, but I had to take time to reflect on the positive things happening. It really took close to a year to see drastic changes in my life, and after that year, I still continue to work on myself and make improvements (we'll talk about how in an upcoming section). This program is in addition to all those bullets I outlined above, but it doesn't have to be overwhelming if you take it at the right speed. Remember, you're going for a life transformation, so take it one step at a time; crawl, walk, and then run. Not only is it less daunting this way, but you'll also be able to conceptualize, implement and process the steps better, in order to create a life-long conversion.

Second:

Ease up yourself on living a 'textbook life'. If you don't get to the dentist one year, just go at the next possible time. If you don't eat as healthy as you could have one day, just try to balance that out another day. Don't beat yourself up for not living a life that is defined on paper as 'perfect'.

Third:

There is no time limit (or predictor) for how long this process will take. It probably took you a long time to get to where you are, just as it took me decades. Nothing happens overnight, so don't set yourself up for disappointment with overinflated expectations. Give yourself time to really understand the different principles before you start jumping on to the next. You are about to go on a journey of exploration of yourself and your surroundings and that will take time to evaluate. You already have a full plate. Don't overwhelm yourself by trying to change your life overnight and tackling all the steps in this book, because it could make you slip backwards. But even if you take two steps forward and one step back before going forward again, you're ahead of the game. Just keep going. Steady wins the race.

I suggest you target completing this journey in 12 months or less. I have seen it happen and I want to share a note of caution: If you take too long and put this book down saying you'll come back to it later, you'll lose traction and you'll lose the potential change in your life. If you are committed to making a change in your life, you can absolutely work these steps in less than a year. If that means you give up some time in your life somewhere else, do it! It will be worth it in the end. This is your life and your happiness we are talking about after all.

Using this program, I picked myself up from off the floor and turned my entire life around. If I can do it, you can do it.

Time to hit RESET

Step 1: Recognize

As Zig Ziglar said, "The first step in solving a problem is to recognize that it does exist."

All too often with the craziness of our days and our busy schedules, we fail to take time to self-reflect. We're usually the last person we consider. In the meantime, life has changed from our kindergarten innocence where we so boldly thought about our needs and loved ourselves to one day you waking up and having no idea who's staring back at you in the mirror.

It is like that idea that if you put a frog into a pot of water and then let it boil, it has no idea what is happening. Because it's so gradual, it doesn't jump out to save itself. That what the lack of self-reflection will do. It's also the thing that will save us.

Therefore, the first step to RESET is to Recognize. This is where you stop romanticizing about what is truly happening in your life, take the blinders off, take a good hard look at yourself, and commit to the new life you are building. Commit to recognizing that person in the mirror again, it all starts here!

Chapter 1: Enough-is-Enough!

There I sat, crouched on my back porch drawing smoke from the lit cigarette pursed between my lips. My phone was blowing up with incessant text messages from friends discussing plans and their outfits for the evening. I grabbed my glass of wine-- it was my fifth. I was convinced I still had life left in me to go out. It was, in fact, only 6:30pm on a Friday night. I didn't want them to know I had been drinking, but how would they? I was fine. My history proved that I couldn't be drunk in public. Nothing good ever came of that. However, I wasn't intoxicated. I could make it to 11pm. I had plenty of life in me. The messages were bouncing faster and faster. How could these girls have so much to talk about? I made my way into the house, stared blankly in my closet at what I would want to wear. My pajamas sounded more appealing than any outfit I would want to wear, so I slipped them on, convinced they wouldn't be my final outfit of the evening. With my boy-shorts and t-shirt, I made my way to the kitchen and topped off my glass of wine telling myself that this one would be the last glass. Any more and they surely would know I had been drinking and I couldn't let them know I drank alone. I suddenly became overwhelmed by the idea of getting ready, made my way back outside and slid my back down the side of my house as I lit a cigarette.

I wasn't a smoker, except when I drank. I drank every day, so you can do the math. I smoked in private, so I really wasn't a smoker. I wasn't a smoker and I wasn't an alcoholic. I hid both, so they didn't exist. But, they did, and my world was split in two; a hard-working businesswoman and an after-hours alcoholic who was scared of herself and ashamed of whom she had become.

Smoke in my lungs helped take my buzz to the next level, and sure enough, by 7:30pm I was almost 2 bottles of wine in with half a pack of cigarettes burned into my lungs since leaving work. Great! Jen, your last glass wasn't your last and now you're far too inebriated to be seen in public. You might as well curl up on your couch because your blackout is just around the corner.

I couldn't really say where this came from, this lifestyle crept up on me. I was the one who was responsive and outgoing, not hiding in her house wearing her pajamas and smashed on a Friday night before the sun went down. I wanted desperately to have a life that I could let someone peer into and be comfortable exposing my full self, but I was ashamed of my 'after-hours' self. The 'day-time' people in my life would have been shocked to know what was really happening.

I didn't want to feel anything, so I didn't. I numbed everything. A compilation of bad decisions, bad choices, physical and mental abuse, and poor body image issues led me to one conclusion -- I didn't want to feel, and I wanted to bury all memories. All my drinking did was cause more bad decisions, bad choices, physical and mental abuse, and unwanted activities. I was in a vortex, a catch 22, and I didn't know how to get out.

Numbing the bad also numbs the good, I had lost the ability to feel many things. I just didn't care. The only feeling I truly felt was anger, hatred and disgust. I was just negative, even if I walked around with a smile. I found I had a wall between me and anyone who was close to me. Dating was almost out of the question. I was too broken to have a healthy relationship and I had too much I was hiding. When I peeled the layers back I was miserable, during and after-hours. I had lost my joy. My addictions had stolen them from me. I'm not sure how I ended up here. It just happened. For years, I acknowledged I had a problem with my life. I knew I needed to make a change, but I didn't know just how badly I had allowed my life to spiral out of my control. It had taken me bit by bit.

I couldn't begin to count the number of 'Day-1's' I had in my life. It seemed every Monday was the promise of a new beginning, and every 'last hoorah' was promised to be my last. Add that up for over more than 15 years, and I can confidently say I spent a large majority of my adult life wanting something different, wanting something more, and never fully committing to stopping myself from my own destructive behavior.

My weekend ended as soon as it began, so goes for getting together with the girls on Friday night. I hadn't even touched base once in the last 48 hours. I was sobering up on Sunday night after another bender weekend. I had been drunk since I left work on Friday, accomplished nothing, and when I wasn't drinking, I was sleeping. I don't know when I began day-drinking, but the downward spiral seemed to go faster once my boundary of not drinking before 5pm got trampled over. That changed to where I woke up in the morning and wanted a drink. I knew as soon as I took a sip of alcohol that I would be unproductive and fall asleep shortly thereafter, so how could a highly motivated, go-getter end up drinking all weekend accomplishing zero? Fortunately, I had kept benders to weekends only. I can only imagine how my life and my drinking would have progressed had I not quit drinking. There I was on Sunday night with the promise of a new life ahead of me because tomorrow was Monday. Monday represented the promise of a new day and a new fresh start -- the end to the madness. Mondays gave hope of a new life without alcohol, this was in fact the last time.

However, Monday always came and went. Every 'last hoorah' became just another day I despised. My life spiraled further and further and the shame kept piling up.

As soon as I left the office on Monday afternoon, I would drive to the store and find myself with a couple of bottles of wine. Two hours later, I would be passed out. How did this happen again? I thought Monday was supposed to bring about a new life. Why do I have no control when I've adamantly told myself that this behavior has to stop? I didn't trust myself anymore with my own empty, failed promises. It seemed the more I wanted a change but couldn't achieve it, the lower I sank in life.

I knew there was more to life than where I was. The fact that I seemed to have no control gnawed at me day-after-day. I knew I had the capacity to do more with my life and to give back and make a difference in this world, yet I felt shackled as a prisoner in my own body. Every day, my frustration and disappointment rose higher as I felt chained to a lifestyle I despised.

As I left work, I slid into my Ford truck with my black-pencil skirt and buttoned up blouse. I slowly took my hair down, exposing the kinks from my hair tie. The day had been a success, I delivered a solid presentation at work and I found out my best friend was having a baby. My brain told me to go home and exercise, but my mind told me to go celebrate. It was always something-- there was always a reason or an excuse to drink, and every day, it was something different. My coworkers thought I was a straightedge, gym advocate. Little did they know where my evening would end and neither did I. I couldn't let them in. God forbid they see what I became-- it could cost me my job. Let them see the put together woman in the office. That's who I wanted to be anyhow. I feared anyone seeing Jen during her bewitching hour.

As I drove home, the maddening conversation convincing myself not to drink ensued in my head. Drink, don't drink, drink, don't drink, it was a tug-of-war game in my head. Tonight, I won! I relished these evenings. I hated drinking, so when I could go home and be at peace, I was elated! I would wake up the next day with ideas of grandeur. I had been cured of the madness! I was no longer held captive to the bonds of addiction, I had a handle on the drinking. It didn't have a handle on me. My sweat in the gym was extra sweet, I was on a new path in life and I was going to take a full advantage. But no sooner would work end that day and I would find myself in the store buying bottles of wine again.

The high of sobriety and the new promise at life had all but fizzled away. I was back to the life I hated. The high was short lived and my spirit was shattered. My hopes had been crushed. I felt like a yo-yo and I was forced to live in silence because of the stigma and shame.

Humiliated. Failure. Worthless. Unworthy. Tainted. Diseased. Scars of shame.

There were many words I could use to describe how I felt about myself. I would often think, "What if my coworkers knew what was in my head? What would my parents do if they knew their daughter wanted to take the life they gave her? How would my friends react if they knew the real truth about my life?" I had bought into the ideology that society has fostered that I was a 'bad person' for my addictions. Believe me, no one wanted change more than I did. I just didn't know how and I was too ashamed to raise my hand for help.

I suppose growing up in a house that looked a little like the Brady Bunch conditioned me to think that life should be picture-perfect. So, in addition to feeling the social stigma of admitting that I was struggling, there was also the cultural stigma I created in my mind from what I observed around me. I felt as though I needed to fit a certain persona, and starting at a young age, I learned to show the world only what I thought they wanted to see. The truth is that I was creating a barrier from having close connections with anyone, and this was just the beginning of keeping every close and personal relationship in my life at arm's length.

At a young age, I wanted to be a Psychologist. I knew I had a passion for helping people, and it was evident by the situations I found myself in. I was always that confidant that people trusted. I was there when people needed me. I was the one that would go the extra mile to help someone. Helping was just in my nature.

It was somewhere along the way that I decided I was going to take a different path. The death of three friends in my senior year of college made me realize you get one life to live so I moved to Italy to live my best life. It was there that I got the phone call that my best friend had committed suicide. It was one more tick mark on the wall of pain I had around my heart. Not only was I surrounded in one of the best places on earth (geographically speaking), but I was also surrounded by inexpensive and readily available wine. I was learning that in addition to the good feeling wine gave, it also numbed my pain. I was fanning the embers in my soul, unaware of the monster I was indulging. All I knew was I felt happy and that's how I wanted to live -- happy.

After a couple of years, I returned to the States and landed a variety of jobs and careers in various cities around the US. During that time, I even found myself married to a gentleman and we both realized that it was not the right fit. I was in different locations (international and domestic). I had a variety of diverse jobs and career tracks. I was married and then quickly divorced. My life was a random maze and I felt like the rat trying to find the cheese. During it all, those embers had turned into a fire and I was unable to put out the flames.

I had no idea where I wanted to be, no idea who I was, no idea what I wanted to do, no idea who I wanted to be around with, and all the while, I was standing on a liquid foundation in my life, quite literally. I never stopped to make time for myself and build a solid foundation. I just kept bouncing around letting life make the calls.

I was impulsive to say the least. I felt a bit like a bull in a China shop aggressively moving through the store of life unaware of the consequences of my actions. My marriage started as a brash decision in a courthouse on the day of one of my many court cases. When my case was dismissed, the court gave us a discount to get married, so we did. I'll never forget calling my parents, neither of whom were surprised. They had become accustomed to my impulsive decision making. It wasn't my intent to live recklessly, but I never took the time to slow down and self-reflect along the way. At some point, a culmination of bobbing and weaving through life brought me to a place I hadn't anticipated to be (drunk, divorced, hospitalized, and jailed, to name a few).

You may not be as reckless as I was or have had the same upbringing, gone through the exact same struggles, or battle the same demons. I do know, however, there are many of us that take a look in the mirror one day and just wonder, "How did I get here?" Whatever brought you here might just be the very reason you picked up this book.

Your story is likely different from mine, but I'll tell you, your motivators are likely the same:

- There is something in your life you that isn't right
- There's someone inside of you that you've become disconnected from
- There's a secret you hide from others (and the fear of being found out)
- You want change in your life but you just don't know how
- There are feelings of inadequacy, hopelessness and a freight train coming right at you

It's normal, it's called life. Life piles on us and what it leaves us with a disconnect from the person within and keeps us from getting the life we desire. The fundamentals of life are the same—even if we have different stories and ways we got to where we are.

I have always kept laser focus on areas around school and work. In fact I believe I tried to compensate for my demons by pouring my blood, sweat and tears into any job I had. I had a solid group of friends and a supportive family. I landed in the great state of Texas, bought a quaint home, and rescued a little girl cat (I named her Booger). I stay active and in shape, and fitness is a huge aspect of my life. Overall, my life doesn't sound too bad! In fact, I have a great life! However, with all this good, I had lost control of an area in my life that was winning the battle in taking my soul. Since I had learned to live two distinct lives at a young age starting at 12 when my eating disorder crept into my life, it was easy to apply this in my adult life.

I always hated the interview question of where I wanted to be in 5 years. Sure, I could come up with something that sounded challenging and ambitious, but the truth was I secretly wondered if I would be living in another 5 years. I had no idea what I had done the night before. How was I to know where I wanted to be in 5 years? I knew I wanted to be happy and healthy but I had no idea how to accomplish that, so coming up with a 5-year work plan was pretty ambitious to pinpoint. It wasn't that I didn't have hopes or dreams, I was just all over the place in my mind with no clear path. I secretly lived a life of being a prisoner in my own skin, so no matter how many times you asked me where I wanted to be in 5 years, I knew in my heart that if I made it in another 5 years, it would be nothing short of a miracle. To say this was a lonely feeling would be an understatement. I was living a lie and it ate at me every day. I was fighting myself internally every day and the madness was building in my mind. The eager young optimistic child inside was losing the battle.

I didn't feel as though I could open up and talk about my struggles. Mainstream society hasn't embraced struggles/anxiety/addiction/mental health as 'dinner time talk'. I bottled up my feelings inside and tried to steer the ship on my own. My world got very dark, yet I tried to face the outside world with a smile. My internal dialogue was abusive and scary, and it's sad and terrifying to think of what was going on in my mind when I felt at my lowest.

What finally did it for me? What made me finally take Day-1 seriously? Like I mentioned before, it all came down to someone telling me I needed to love myself. It wasn't the egregious bottoms I had, it was actually a man I was dating that cared enough to tell me that I needed to learn to love myself. It wasn't an earth-shattering statement, but it came at just the right time that I needed to hear it. When we were sitting down and having 'the talk', I had some sort of spiritual awakening in my soul and I knew it was time, I had enough with the madness.

I wish I had that moment on camera, because I am pretty certain I froze in time as I watched the WD-40 loosen the gears in my head. I wonder what this gentleman was thinking as I was processing those 7 sweet words, "You need to learn to love yourself." I am usually pretty quick with words, but I remember vividly sitting there motionless while I imagined being completely alone for the rest of my life. I envisioned myself as a young child with hope and a future, none of which had come to fruition. All the times I played house growing up would never become more than role play. I wasn't destined to spend a life of happiness with a partner. I was slave to a poison I despised, and I couldn't feel any love or think about my future. The gears were now in full motion in my brain and I finally said, "Enough is enough," and this time something different happened inside of me and I meant it.

Change doesn't happen by chance, it happens when you make the change. You no longer have any more 'last hoorahs'. Today is your Day-1. Today is the day you commit to hitting the reset button on your life, no matter how big or how small it may be. When you commit to saying enough-is-enough and you take the content of this book, and really meditate on the principles and implement them, your change will come.

If you truly commit to yourself and this holistic program then I will tell you that it will be the best journey you will ever take. I made a commitment to myself that I would do whatever it took to reclaim my life, and in true addict form, I took resetting and reclaiming my life intentionally and intensely. I became addicted to my transformation and in a good way! Throughout my journey, I documented the steps I took to get to where I am today, and I want to share that with you so you too can reclaim your life and love the person staring back at you in the mirror. Have you had enough that you're finally ready to commit to the changes you need to reclaim your life? Tomorrow is not guaranteed so if you are waiting for the 'right time', the time is now.

It has now become my life purpose to help you through sharing my journey. There were days I didn't believe that I could do it, but now I have become the person I have always known I could be. I continue to challenge myself and aspire to be better than I was yesterday, even exceeding my own expectations. I look at my scars and how they've strengthened me and made me into the person I am today.

I look back at all the times I told myself Monday was the start of Day 1, but I knew I really didn't mean it. I would just break that promise to myself again and it almost became a habit that was no big deal. And what I know in this process is that even though that gentleman spoke those seven life changing words to me, he couldn't want the change for me more than I did. I was the only one responsible for it. I had to be committed. I had to truly want it. I had to own my own transformation.

I said it before, and I'll say it again, my journey is not necessarily your journey but the steps to success I took can apply to yours. What I have learned in opening up and speaking out is that so much of the human experience is the same. We share so many commonalities across our lives. At the end of the day, we all have feelings, hopes, and desires, we want happiness, and peace. Our stories *will* vary, but at our core, **we are all riding the same train of life, we just have different views from our cabin.**

As you read on, don't work each chapter all at once. Start by taking one principle at a time to really understand and have it sink in. Only when I was making good progress with one principle, would I start to work on another area, until I found I could juggle multiple areas at the same time. Don't dive in and do them all at the same time. You need to start at the beginning and set your foundation. Your first step is to say, "Enough is enough," and commit to something different. Today is Day-1. Are you with me? Let's do this!

~~~~~

- No one can make you want to change, it boils down to you.
- If you are wanting change then it's time to say enough-is-enough.
- Enough-is-enough is a commitment that you are done with what you want to change.

Chapter 2: Getting Honest

I always answered the salutation of, "How's it going?" with the generic answer, "Great -- living the dream!" I don't know how many times I've said this to people, but I was not living the dream. On the outside, it wasn't too far-fetched of a response. I had a good job, a house, a nice truck, and I traveled the globe. I had a truly rich life of experiences. But I was hollow inside. I was ashamed of the double-life I was living. I was unable to get close to people. I hated whom I had become. I had no control over my addiction, and it was a matter of time before I ended up in prison or dead. I saw the freight train coming at me and I couldn't slow it down. Living the dream? It certainly didn't seem like it when I closed my eyes at night. I couldn't admit to my friends or family what was happening, and most of all, I wasn't admitting to myself what was really happening inside my head. I just felt torn apart and was a victim day-in-day-out. I never asked myself in the morning what I wanted. I never stopped to think about where I was in life. I didn't think about the future. I just kept moving like a zombie through life, directionless. Birthdays sped up year-after-year, and I was racing through life, aging before my eyes, lying all the way, and far from being honest.

Time is one thing we can never get back, so use it effectively. It's time to get honest.

What's really going on? What are you sick and tired of?

When you are alone in your thoughts, what don't you want others to know? When you read the last chapter, what went through your mind? Who do you believe you are when no one is looking? You may not have all the answers, but if you have one area to start with, one thing you can identify that needs to be changed, then you have a place to start. You might not know where you want to be but knowing that one thing is a good place to start. If you're with me, so far you've committed to saying enough-is-enough and now it's time to get honest.

I knew I wanted happiness and that's a broad and vague goal. I knew more specifically that my drinking was holding me back in all areas of my life. As I went along my journey, I found so much more that needed to be addressed, but I committed to change and I committed to stop drinking. It may sound simple, but it was a direction and a brilliant place to start.

You will also uncover more about yourself as you progress in your journey, but you have to start somewhere, so just pick something. It doesn't really matter how big or how small as long as you're moving in the right direction.

Making these changes in your life could very well impact all areas (friends, family, social situations, jobs, places, things, and in a very positive way, your health, wealth and love). Rightfully so, this can be a little overwhelming to think about. That's why I don't want you to get too far ahead of yourself. Don't try to puzzle the final picture together in your head and don't anticipate what the situation will look like. Don't guess what others will perceive. Let it happen as it happens. The only thing I want you to think of is the feeling you'll have when you get there -- the elation, the happiness, the peace, and the joy. THAT is something that you can look forward to and anchor in.

For you to make the level of change you want in your life, you need to get honest with yourself. There may be a lot of shame, guilt, anger, frustration and pain around what you find. I want you to take this and fuel yourself as we dig in and start to make the changes you want to achieve. If you aren't getting real with yourself, then you are cutting corners. If you cut corners, your end product will suffer as a result. Have you ever moved into a house and you saw where the builder used cheap materials or tried to cover something up with some caulk or paint? Don't compromise the quality of your end product (or make it impossible to achieve) because you are cutting corners or not getting real with yourself. It's to your benefit to have the tough conversations with yourself, because nobody else is going to do it for you.

Let's get started.

Let's first set a few ground rules.

1. Change doesn't happen by chance
2. Your past doesn't define you
3. Hardship builds character
4. You have the power within
5. Self-reflection is a necessity
6. You have to get honest with yourself
7. You can change your destiny
8. Tough decisions are coming ahead
9. Listen to your gut instinct
10. You will get through this
11. Your life and your mind can change if you make it happen
12. Everything is subject to change

Go back and reference these because these are some of the key fundamentals to the success of this journey. I want you to be successful and it comes from within, so dig deep, get raw with yourself, and don't try to fool yourself. Follow your gut if it starts speaking to you.

Think about what is happening in your life, in your behavior, in your mindset that you know you want to change. It might be a behavior, ideology, activity, or maybe even a person. Think big and broad as you walk through these questions. Write down what comes to your mind. You need to see these on paper. `

- WHAT:
    - What in your life, do you feel you have lost all control over?
    - What is happening in your life that is making you unhappy?
    - What in your life, do you feel is out of sync with who you are in your core?
    - What do you feel in your life is controlling you?
    - What in your life is the black cloud that keeps following you around that keeps raining on your parade and you just want to be out from under it?
    - What do you feel is holding you back from being the best person you can be?
    - What do you keep telling yourself that starting Monday you won't do again?
    - What are you just flat out sick of justifying to others and yourself?
    - What are you trying to hide from others so they don't see?
    - What are you doing in your life you know you shouldn't be doing?
    - What aren't you doing in your life that you think you should be doing?

Ouch, I know. Even writing these questions and having gone through a lot of healing in my life, it still drums up some heavy feelings. Being truthful and honest here is going to help bring you clarity so take them seriously. Go back through them again and think about each one.

Now, let's address the HOW.

- HOW:
    - How do you feel when you engage in these behaviors, activities, beliefs?
    - How do you impact others?
    - How has this behavior impacted your own life?
    - How has your life spiraled from where you envisioned it?

- How many times have you had a Day-1 and for what?

If your answers to these questions are negative in nature, then it should be clear as day that you need to commit to change. If you want to be free from whatever bondage is holding you down and ruining your life, sharpen that pencil and start taking notes.

I punted these questions down the road for so many years. I knew the answer, or so I thought. I had to rid myself of the addictive behaviors that held me captive, then I would be happy and free. I would jump from one addiction to another; albeit food, to smoking, to alcohol, to caffeine and so on. They controlled almost all aspects of my life, but I kept telling myself that this was the last hoorah and Monday would be a new beginning. I would give myself a timeframe of when my new life would start and guess what? I was never really committed to doing it, so it never happened.

It seems so easy for someone on the outside to say 'just stop drinking', or 'just stop eating', 'or just stop gambling', or 'just be happy', or 'stop judging others', or 'just love your job for what it is', or 'just let something go.' But if you are living a life where you feel you have lost control, if you feel somehow powerless in the situation, and if you feel that you have some connection with the behavior because it gives you comfort (even if you ultimately hate it), then it's not so easy to 'just stop' one hundred percent. I also know how frustrating it is. I know how it feels to not know how to change it. If I understood moderation, then I would have done it but I'm an addict and moderation is not a concept my brain recognizes. Words are easy -- I get it!

If you were struggling to answer some of the questions and you don't know what is wrong but you know something isn't right, that's okay too. As you go through this book and get real with yourself, you are going to start addressing behaviors that are going to uncover areas you might not even know were dysfunctional. As long as you are committed to improving your life, as long as you want to live your best life, and as long as you know you are committed to striving for happiness, then that is base enough for this journey.

Now, you may have picked up the book thinking you know what it is that you want or need to change. I knew I had to stop drinking. It was going to kill me if I didn't. What I didn't know was that my drinking was only a mere symptom of the problem and not the problem itself. I didn't know this at first and you may not realize what the problem is that you're facing. I'll give you a hint -- it's inside of you that needs to be addressed. My symptoms went away when I addressed the problem, me. At least I knew enough to know that I needed areas of my life to change and it didn't matter that I didn't know everything. All I needed from myself was commitment and honesty.

> *I THOUGHT I had one behavior to change and resolving that problem would make me whole. I couldn't have been further from accurate. Spoiler alert -- there is likely more than one area you need to address and I tell you this not to disappoint you, but so that you are prepared. It's normal! Because so many times when we solve one problem in life, another one may appear.*

Now that you've written down some of the behaviors that you no longer want in your life, let's walk through some questions to help you think about where you want to be. This is merely an activity to get you thinking of the future even if you don't know exactly what it will look like. As you go through this, you may change your mind about what you think fits best. Remember, life not a straight line, your path is likely to change along the way.

I want you to think about what it might look like for you to achieve happiness (again, this is just your perception today).

- What makes you happy (minimum 3 things)?
- When do you feel you are at your best?
- Where do you see yourself in the future (doing, living, etc.)?
- What does your happy place look like?

- What does achieving your goal(s) look like to you?

As you progress through this book, you will find that you move forward faster by being honest. And this is a no judgment zone -- you don't get to judge yourself for what you want or what makes you happy. They are mere facts. If the latest trend in coffee doesn't make you happy, it doesn't make you happy. You don't have to pretend to like it to be a cool kid. You already are a cool kid. If you want a truck (like me) then you want a truck. You don't have to force yourself to like fancy car instead.

You get to be you. You get to love all of you and you get to do it unapologetically.

It's critical that you self-reflect and really take the time to assess the answers to these questions. You don't have to share them with others, but I want you to write them down and then read through the answers.

What I want you to take from this section is to start to get the gears turning and assessing what is really happening inside of you. I want you also start opening your mind that there may be more that will be uncovered and it's okay that they aren't listed as what needs to change or even what makes you happy. Everything is subject to change. Remember that rule.

~~~~~

- In order to achieve real change in your life, you have to get honest. This may uncover pain, discomfort, tears, anger, but your honesty will get you the real results you are looking for!
- You created a list, but know that everything is subject to change.

- If you are not honest then you are hurting your progress.

Chapter 3: No More Excuses, No More Victim Mindset!

There always seemed to be some excuse I could find to lean on. Anything could be an excuse. It didn't have to be significant. The fact that I had the 'case of the Mondays' was excuse enough. I could have had a hard day at work, a bad date, a long commute home, been mad at myself for having done something, or mad at the fact that a passing train held my life up for an additional 5 minutes on my way home. God forbid something or anything make me unhappy. It gave me an excuse to justify my behaviors.

I was a queen of excuses, and the only person I was making excuses to was myself so they didn't even have to pass a sniff test. It's not like the teacher was going to knock points for my having a bad excuse for why I didn't do my homework. No, I made excuses to justify my behavior and my actions, and whatever I came up with was good enough for me.

These excuses became my scapegoat -- the blame and reasoning for all my wrongdoings, my faults and subpar behavior. I could lean on these reasons and I was constantly pointing fingers and justifying the reasoning for my behavior, never taking ownership.

Have you ever been around someone that is always blaming others for their actions? Maybe you have a coworker that is constantly coming up with an excuse for missing their deliverables. These people are incapable of showing real results and 'big-win' progress because they are constantly the victim of their world showing a lack of accountability for the deliverable they are responsible for. Instead of self-reflecting and taking ownership of their world, they point fingers, never taking into account the role they play in their own success. In a sense, that's how I was. I never stopped to look at my situation. I just blamed everything around me. I used all those situations to somehow validate the reason for my behavior and yet I was always the common denominator in the equation, never taking ownership.

It's very possible you don't have a vice you cling to that you need an excuse to justify, but I don't doubt that you are making excuses to justify something in your life -- behavior, communications, attitude, level of patience, or negativity. There is something in your life that you're making excuses for and I'll tell you, it needs to stop.

You may not even realize you have crutches you lean on, so you may need to dig deep and start to look at your circumstances in order to see what kind of dependencies you have.

1. Do you justify your behavior by placing blame on any person, place or thing?
2. Do you harbor any ill feelings against someone or something that you keep referencing in your life as a reason for you to justify a behavior?
3. Do you have fear in your life and use an excuse not to face it (fear of making mistakes, fear of what you may uncover, fear of the truth, fear of pain)?
4. Do you constantly defer responsibility of actions away from yourself and project those on to a person, place, or thing?
5. Do you lack goals, so you find yourself not making real progress in your life?

6. Are you wrapped up in a lifestyle or mindset that you know isn't for you and it has taken over your life?
7. Do you lack motivation to even want to make a change so you just make excuses instead?

An excuse is not always, "I'm late because of an accident on the way to work." An excuse can be that you are afraid of what you'll find out, afraid of what you'll feel, or maybe you just flat out lack the motivation to want to make a change. Whatever is your reason, you're about to cut out all those excuses.

For me, every one of those reasons applied. Something aggravated me and that was my excuse. I didn't want to face my fears and that was my excuse. I didn't want to feel pain and that was my excuse. My brain was held captive by an addiction and my disease was my excuse. I'm referring to it as an excuse but you may call it a justification, a reason, or a rationalization. They all have the same meaning and effect. I wasn't striving for change and I didn't have tangible goals that I made actionable. It was like being scared and directionless, while pointing fingers at everyone else in my life. I knew that all that needed to change.

When you look at all the situations in your life around the area you are blaming:

- WHOM did you place the blame on?
- WHAT was the situation?
- WHY did you place the blame and why was it their fault?
- WHERE is your ownership or WHERE could you have done something different in the situation?

Don't get stuck here, just start to identify where you are placing blame and making excuses on people, places or things.

Before we wrap up this principle, start to be mindful of when you are placing blame on feelings. I was depressed, I hated myself, I hated my life, I was lonely, I was frustrated, I was sad, and all of those feelings I used as excuses. Here's the kicker: I was depressed so I drank and my drinking made me depressed. It was a vicious cycle that I had to rip in half. Equally as sabotaging to yourself is playing a victim.

Stop playing the victim

It was always 'poor me'. The world was against me and it seemed that everything was 'woe-is-me' and I was the victim in every situation. If someone was walking slowly in front of me, I'd let out a silent sigh, roll my eyes and spew something in my brain like 'thanks for slowing ME down'. If I went on a bad date, the world must have been communicating to me that I was surely going to be alone and miserable forever! If my coffee wasn't stocked on the store shelf, I would say, "Of course, life never goes my way!" Looking at those everyday examples exemplifies the level of victim I felt I was, in my own world. The world was clearly against me in any and every situation. Nothing went my way. I think of Eeyore in Winnie the Pooh. He was the epitome of a victim, always expecting misfortune to happen. I found myself adopting that frame of mind all too often. I was playing on the defense.

Oh and for sure, nothing was ever my fault. Nothing was my responsibility, even the thoughts that went through my head.

One of my first real jobs after college was working with a company that contracted with the Federal Government. They had hired me as an IT recruiter working on government contracts. I was brought over as a referral and I was brought in to help clean up the department. I had zero recruiting experience. In fact, I look back at some of the conversations I had with candidates and literally, I made no sense. No one trained me and no one taught me. I was just given access to job descriptions and a data base of candidates and this company allowed someone to talk to real people with zero knowledge of what I was talking about. It was probably a decision the company should have thought a bit deeper about.

I didn't do poorly. I actually did quite well considering I was learning on the fly -- I'm a smart gal and can adapt and learn quickly. After a few months, they decided to bring on another recruiter and I prepared her offer letter as directed by my boss. I was in total shock, as she was making 60% more than I was and she was the exact same age! I wanted to like this new girl and I did, but I couldn't get over the fact that she was making so incredibly much more money than I was! Why on earth would my boss have allowed me to prepare the offer letter of my peer, at the same level as me, and for me to see the salary which was grossly inequitable to mine?

It was hard for me not to make the situation about me. I felt as though I had been wronged. I'm not going to deny that there was some level of discussion that we could have about the fact that I should have been paid more, but I made the entire situation about me -- the poor victim. I never took into perspective the benefits of the job that I was getting that would carry me throughout my career. I overlooked the fact that I had taken a hiatus after college and went to live in Italy while my peers were starting their careers. My peer had a couple years of experience and it turned out I could actually learn from her. I was given the same title as someone that had far more experience, which could have held weight if I stayed in that line of work. I overlooked the fact that I had this amazing resume-building experience and actually ended up obtaining a top secret security clearance, which allowed me to get a job in Operations, that ultimately was my ticket to start contracting with the government, which ultimately led me to Afghanistan, where I spent an incredible year of my life! But, woe-is-me, I was too fixated on being the victim to be grateful for what I had, to be present in the moment, and enjoy the journey.

When we are the victim, we are blaming someone else as opposed to taking ownership over our situation. Not everything that happens to you may appear fair, but there could also be something much larger that is happening. You may be going through a trial so you can come out stronger or more well-rounded on the other end. There may be a reason at a more macro level that you are not getting what you are asking for. It's not that you are a victim, you are merely not ready for what you are asking for (such as me and my dating life which I kept asking for but I was in no way ready to have someone in my life -- I was a broken mess).

I especially know from an addict's perspective that it's easy to blame others for your lot in life and turn to a bottle for comfort. I was so good at losing myself in one world just so I could forget the other. Underneath that, you might be surprised to know that I was getting something that felt deceivingly positive out of being a victim and this is why it can be so hard to change this mentality.

So you may ask, "What could I possibly be getting that was positive out of feeling like a victim?" I could blame someone or something else instead of taking ownership of my own situation. I didn't need to confront myself with the idea that I needed to change. It became the world's responsibility to change instead. I gave myself sympathy and sometimes others would give me sympathy too if I shared that awful thing that happened to me. I continued to romanticize the life I was living instead of getting honest with myself. I could continue to make excuses and I was allowed to hold on to my anger.

It's all a mindset, a perception, and this perception creates our reality. Have you ever talked with a child that has an imaginary friend? You may look at the child and not see the friend, but to this child the friend exists. That is the child's reality, not yours, but the perception of the situation the child has created in his/her mind. When I did my first body building competition, I didn't win first place, but I was the biggest winner on the stage. How? I had overcome an eating disorder and I suffer from Body Dysmorphic Disorder. I cringe at the thought of being in a bathing suit. It is not an area I feel any level of comfort. I don't see what others see, and it's something I've had to manage since I became cognizant of the detrimental impact it can have on my health and life. I stood on stage as a 6'1" woman in 5" heels in a tiny bikini, and I showed off all the hard work I had done to sculpt my body. I wasn't perfect and the competition wasn't about that for me. It was about getting out there and having self-confidence to face my biggest fear. I stood 6'6" in the air and I remember my legs shaking as I was so nervous, but I did it. I freaking did it! I could have been hard on myself for not winning, or I could have been hard on myself because it's very difficult for us tall people to get ripped (more space to cover), or I could have criticized myself for any number of little details, but I chose to perceive myself as a winner.

In order for you to be successful on this journey, you need to take ownership of your situation. You can only control you so that's your focus from now on. Your thoughts, actions, perception, and mind -- you own those. If you tell yourself you are a victim, then you'll be a victim. If you want to be a winner, then you need to tell yourself that you are, in fact, winning! It's finding the good in situations. It's being content right where you are at. It's accepting what you do not control and it's diverting your brain to a positive frame of mind when you start to go to a dark place.

I want you to write a list of every place you feel you are a victim.

I feel a victim in ____(this situation)_____, because __(put your reasoning here)_____.

Think of work, home, relationships, situations, and wherever you believe you are being victimized.

Now, take another color out and write another list. List the situation with another explanation that takes you out of being the victim.

Here's an example:

I feel a victim at work because my coworker got the promotion, but I know I deserved it.

Spin this around: I didn't get a promotion at work, and

- I still have a lot to learn before taking on that level of responsibility
- Another door is bound to open
- I have too many other things to focus on right now anyhow
- My coworker is doing a great job
- I'm learning a lot

If you catch yourself saying, "Of course this would happen to me," or "I can never win," or "When will things go my way?" then you are playing the victim. Catch yourself when you are having a pity party and saying one of these phrases (and there are many more examples) and go through the exercise above. If you continue to position yourself where you constantly feel attacked, then you are limiting your success. You'll learn to adopt a positive perspective on life and as you progress through this book you'll be learning to work on letting go of what you cannot control, you'll start to see how all the concepts in this book intertwine.

For so many years I asked, "Why me?" when I looked at my addiction. Why did it appear that some people, including people in my family, had life so easy and yet, here I was burdened with a disease that was crippling me? My perception of my addiction was defensive. It was like the world was throwing daggers at me and I was struggling just to keep my head up some days. There were many days I just wanted to hide from the world. Many days where I wanted to turn the clock back to when I was 12 and my eating disorder started or to when I was 14 and I had my first drink and just start over. Many days I wanted to be 'normal', and I just wanted to be happy. This addiction -- screw it. I hate what it did to me. However, what did it do for me? I wouldn't be writing this book had it not been for my addiction, I would not have been able to help others through my story, and I would not have become the incredible person I am today had I not gone through the ringer. It's a perception and it's yours to control.

This-is-me or Woe-is-me.

Own it or let it own you.

You are no longer a victim.

As of today, that stops.

First, decide that victimhood doesn't serve you. Take what life hands you with grace and gratitude. Stop making situations all about you. Pull yourself out of being the victim and create a new view of the world where you don't take the perspective of Eeyore. You are on the offensive now and you'll push past situations with positivity and let go of what you cannot control. You will no longer place blame on others. You will take ownership over your life. You hold the keys to your kingdom and if you want to truly be the king or queen, then you need to take responsibility for your land.

There are no more excuses, there is no more victim. Start to pay attention to when you are making justifications or placing blame on others for your behavior and put the kibosh on that way of thinking immediately. If you want change in your life, if you want to find peace and sleep better at night, if you want the opportunity to achieve the love in your life you know you deserve, and if you want the void in your life to be fulfilled, then you have to take responsibility for every area and aspect of your life. There are no more excuses or playing the victim at this point. You've said enough is enough and you're getting honest. Now you're done with finding that scapegoat. It doesn't exist anymore and you can't lean on it to get you out of your jams.

~~~~

- You are responsible for your own life, no one else is to blame.
- Excuses and playing a victim takes ownership and power away from you.
- Being a victim introduces negativity into the situation.
- Do not allow yourself to play the victim anymore -- take ownership from here on out.
- This is your life, your responsibility. No one can take your happiness, your power, or your life from you if you don't let them.
- Eliminating excuses will give you more happiness, create a life you are proud of, allow you to love yourself and be in your power.

Chapter 4: Meditating & Turning to a Higher Power

Meditating and connecting with a higher power was a cornerstone in reclaiming power over my life. I know the concept of a higher power can be controversial to some, but the moment I gave over control, my life began to get under control.

First, I acknowledge there are many forms of a higher power. Secondly, I know there are many different ways in which people connect with their higher power. I'm not here to tell you with who or what, I'm suggesting you open your mind to a being that is higher and greater than you. This being not only has your best interest at all times, but is also able to see the big picture surrounding you. This power will allow challenges in your life to teach you, which if you're willing to learn and accept, will strengthen you throughout your life. This higher power is your guide, your confidant, a force greater than you that doesn't judge and loves you unconditionally.

My higher power is God.

You don't have to be religious to fit this chapter into your life. Meditating will help you focus and connect with that power. What I'm encouraging you to do is find time where you can be alone with your thoughts and bring your strengths, weaknesses, situations, your good and your bad all to the table and work on them in silence. This can be in your car, before you go to bed, on your lunch break, while you're on the toilet, in the shower or wherever. Carve out some time and just stop and get still in your thoughts.

The actual act of prayer or meditation doesn't have one format or definition, but it does require you to get into your own thoughts and get quiet. It's about getting honest-- addressing where you are truly at, what you need, what you are grateful for, asking for help, asking for guidance, and most of all, listening for a response. I am constantly asking to be placed where my skills can be of maximum benefit, and I have to be ok with the response.

Prayer and meditation are talking to, communicating with, and listening to your higher power. It's getting quiet enough to listen. It's being open enough to talk. It's being mindful of what is happening around you. It's asking for guidance and direction. It's like talking with your best friend. Sometimes you just want an ear to listen. Because your higher power has your best interest in mind, it knows what is coming in the future, what is good for you, and are able to guide you even when you cannot see it. Therefore, when you meditate and pray, and sit quietly enough to listen, you'll hear the answer for what you need. Tests and trials may come as part of navigating to your target. It's all part of the process to the end state and guided by your higher power.

Remember the Garth Brooks song, 'Unanswered Prayers'? It's about a man thanking God for not answering his prayer to get a particular woman in his life. If he had, then he never would have been with the true love of his life. Just because something appears unanswered doesn't mean that it's not being answered. It's just being answered in a different way. We need to get quiet and have this dialogue. We need to listen and it might not always be clear. Most of all, we need to have faith that even when we can't make sense of what is happening, that our higher power, who is in control, knows and sees the positive outcome we can't see, and knows what's best for us. Because of this, you can trustingly give that level of control over the situation.

When I started to connect with my higher power, it was like a switch was flipped and I started to see things move and change in my life. I had said enough-was-enough, I committed to honesty, eliminated excuses, and I now was committing to give my life and my situation over to my higher power. It was here that my life began transforming even more before my eyes, and things started to line up that in no way I could have made happen or ever imagined. I asked for my addiction to go away and it did. I asked for my cravings to go away and they did. I asked for direction and purpose in my life and opportunities started to unveil. I was asking, I was listening, I was doing, and my life was changing.

My whole life, I chose what I was doing, when I was doing it, and how I was doing it. I didn't ask for guidance from anyone; higher power, friend, or coach. I had no guidance on a bigger picture and I also wasn't seeking support where I needed it. Not all decisions were bad, but I had created a life that was entirely unsustainable. I was utterly depressed, I had no idea where I was headed and I had given over the power of my mind to a force that was tearing me up. I had to open up myself and get honest with everything that was happening and learn to give it over to my higher power. I ask for direction, guidance, peace, discernment in all that I do, and I give thanks and ask for forgiveness when I've done wrong.

When we have this level of self-awareness and intimacy, then we open ourselves up for improvement. My higher power can see the bigger picture. I cannot, so I have to have faith that what is happening is for a reason. You are human, so not everything will make sense at a micro level for why it is happening. I believe there is truly a greater picture at hand, and at a macro level, all of these pieces of our lives take us to where we need to be. I didn't think my life of pain, agony and addiction was great at the time. I felt like a victim for so many years. I lived in a constant state of depression. I've come to realize that those experiences gave me strength, courage, understanding, an appreciation for life, and the ability to love myself and others. On top of all that, they gave me a story of strength and hope that I can share with you so that you can draw strength from it. I had to realize at the macro level that my higher power was positioning me to become a warrior for others and for myself. I just couldn't see this while I was steering my own ship against a current. It took me getting quiet and honest to really see what was happening.

As I began to meditate, I started to pay close attention to what was happening around me. There were things I may have prayed for that came to fruition, things I prayed for that did not. I was watching for any connections, paying extra attention for the series of events that would happen after a prayer seemed to go unanswered. You see, my idea of a higher power was fairly narrow, I asked for something and I wanted to receive. Even though I had heard about a 'master plan', my focus on life was not as broad and I needed to expand my mind. Instead of getting frustrated with my prayers not being answered (or what appeared to go unanswered), I decided to take an outsider's perspective of my life and try to see the pieces of the puzzle that were being put together.

For someone wanting and needing change in a major way, patience was a challenge. I spent decades running from feelings. Any goal I would make, at the time, I only focused on the end state. Now, I'm was sitting in a pool of feelings, trying to live for the moment, and waiting for my higher power to decide when it was the 'right time' for something to happen, or maybe I'd be led down a path that would have me hit a brick wall so it would teach me a lesson.
SERIOUSLY?! Is that what it was all about to get sober, have a higher power, and let go? Yes, yes it is.

I had to feel it all, experience the wins and the losses. I had to pick myself up off the floor, I had to keep my head high, I had to go through the feelings, I had to listen and pray, and I had to open myself up and admit that my life is better off in His hands. I did all this while I was getting sober and detoxing.

During the first six months of my sobriety, I decided I wanted to go back to school for a PhD and I started down a long 9-month journey of taking GRE prep courses, getting letters of recommendation, gathering sample writing, finding all my old transcripts and everything else required to get into a program. It was not only a lot of money, but it also took a lot of my time. I had done my due diligence and researched which program would suit my desired study. I had interviewed the school before they ever interviewed me. I was confident in my decision, and felt they were confident about me since I made it to the last round of interviews. I was traveling for work when I found out that I had hit that brick wall after 9 months. I received a letter stating I didn't get into the program.

Back when I was in the driver's seat, I would have looked at this situation with anger and disappointment but having committed to allowing my higher power to lead, I took what felt like a punch to the gut and determined there was a larger picture at play. I'm glad I did, because just like Garth Brook's song, I was glad this was an unanswered prayer. I had so much happening in my life, and financially I had made other commitments, leaving not much room or desire to take out such a large loan for school. Additionally, I needed to focus on my own journey. I had committed to learning to love myself. I had no business piling a distraction on top of what I needed to do. Lastly, I would have needed to move and that would have taken me further from my church which I needed to be close to.

Applying to school gave me purpose, a focus, and it helped keep me busy as I was learning to adapt to a new routine after-hours without drinking. Prepping for the GRE gave my brain a challenge it craved and I needed stimulation as my pathways were rebuilding. All-in-all, it was right decision to apply to school, and I am also grateful I did not get in the program. My higher power knew it before I did. I probably would not have written this book when I did because I would have been too busy writing papers.

There is nothing about the situation that I look back at in anger. In fact, it's quite the opposite. I look back at those 9 months as purposeful and strengthening. It wasn't a brick wall, it was a path on my journey. Sometimes, when things appear unanswered, they were intended for a different purpose than what we had anticipated, and we need to accept those lessons as blessings!

I could make a distinct correlation throughout my lifetime when things were on the upswing. I was in meditation and communication with my God. When my life was spiraling downward and seemingly out of control, I had little to no communication with my God. This was a cyclical pattern that I experienced for decades and even though I found peace, comfort and always benefited from having a higher power in my life, I always seemed to revert to trying to run my life without any consultation.

The yo-yo'd communication allowed me to see the two distinct variations in my life. It showed me how dark life could get when I tried to do everything on my own. It also allowed me to experience freedom when I let go and gave it over. There was, without a doubt, a correlation when I was in meditation with my life being good.

What I won't lead you to believe is that finding a relationship with your higher power is going to bring you all happy and uplifting moments. Even now, I don't walk on pink clouds, life isn't handed to me on a silver platter, and I go through my fair share of challenges because it's not a magic genie lamp. The difference now is the way I view those challenges. I believe I'm given trials to mold me into a better person, even to draw me closer to relying on my higher power to help in guiding me, instead of my being the victim in life's reality show. However, it's not just learning lessons and molding me where I benefit, it's undeniable that opportunities are presenting themselves and my life is unveiling and falling into place.

I am constantly asking to be shown where I can be of maximum service. I ask for this daily and I'm open to whatever the direction may be. I ask for discernment, so I can be certain I am hearing the right message. The response I received over and over is to take my story and help transform the lives of others. That's scary and intimidating. For over two decades, I kept a part of myself hidden and now God wants me to broadcast it? What about my family, my friends, and my career? What will people think? What will people say? What if I lose my job? What if people disown me? The voice I kept hearing was to keep moving and that's what I'm doing. It was the magazine, the radio, the speaking gigs, the blogs, the coaching, and the book. These opportunities started to all fall in my lap. I started to receive feedback from the community about how my story was helping to give strength, courage, encouragement, and hope. I was holding back what my higher power knew I possessed, and I had to give over my fears and let Him take them where he needed them, He did and He's doing it.

As with any relationship, it needs water in order to grow. You don't shake someone's hand and immediately know everything about them, or connect on a deep level and have memories! It takes time and effort to get to know each other and know the likes and dislikes to make memories. There is no magic switch that you turn on and 'you're there'. This is where the watering needs to take place.

One of my best friends in Dallas and I have a truly amazing connection that took years to build. She can literally fill in the blanks when I ask her to guess what I'm doing, where I am, or who I'm with. We can banter on a deep or surface level and have an understanding of each other. Although we don't see each other daily, we remain active in each other's lives by communicating via text and other technology mediums. This consistent dialogue back and forth is our water and we've grown this spunky friendship into some real fun banter that keeps us both coming back for more! Who knew that cats and GIF's could be so entertaining, but we've enhanced our relationship by finding the commonalities that we both can appreciate! It's the same when connecting with any person, place, or thing -- it takes time and investment to nurture into something greater.

When I was deep in my addiction, it was not as though I was

never in communication with my higher power, it was just very sporadic communication, VERY sporadic. I would reach out when I needed something, not just to check in and express gratitude for everything I've been blessed with. I never asked for direction, I only prayed when I needed something specific to happen.

Imagine if you had someone in your life that only called you if he/she wanted money or a favor. You see the phone ring, and you know what is coming once you pick up the phone. I don't want to be this person, I don't want to only come asking for things, and yet that is about 99.5% of how all my communications went. Relationships are a give and take. There is a natural ebb and flow that happens in the universe (which we'll mention again in some of the chapters). I needed to be more giving if I wanted to start receiving more blessings. Think of it like your significant other. You cannot expect to be the only one giving to the relationship. One-sided relationships aren't healthy relationships after all.

In addition to meditating, I started filling my ears with sermons. I found a pastor I could relate with and began to listen to his app every day as I drove to work. This ritual helped me to build out a relationship and get to better understand the person I was connecting with in my private time (it also helped to distract me from getting angry while I was driving in traffic). I found that doing this every day helped to make the relationship routine, instead of just 'checking in' when I needed something.

My RESET was a drastic life change for me. I was overcoming a power that had taken control of me for many years -- a power that controlled my thoughts, my mind, my actions, and it covered up the pain I was trying to suppress. It was coming to grips with someone I had grown to hate, and all the while, I had to remain consistent at work. Although I know I am very capable at taking on different roles and wearing many hats, as ambitious as I can be, I also know that I was pretty fragile in the beginning, and my higher power knew that. I believe you won't be given more than you can handle and that certainly held true in this example. As much as I wanted to go back to school, that would have been more than I could have handled. A picture of my life was coming together, I just couldn't see it, and I don't know that I'll ever have the full picture. I have to remain patient, positive, and trust it is evolving as it is supposed to, I'm learning the lessons I need to, and my higher power has it all under control.

I prayed for strength, for my life back, for guidance, for discernment, for the right people to be in my life, for my health, for my leadership, for my friends, for my family, and for breaking the bonds to hell that held me captive. I threw my entire life into this quiet time and allowed myself to open up and get honest. I explicitly gave over the control. "Show me, guide me, take me, it's all yours. Take it. Use it" I didn't want to force myself into the life I thought I should be living. I wanted God to help guide me where I needed to be, which meant listening and giving up control.

Where do you start?

- I suggest you find a quiet space and open your mind to something greater than yourself.
- Self-reflect about where you are in life, where you struggle, what went well in your day, areas you want to do better in, what you are grateful for, what made you happy, what made you sad, and get honest with yourself.
- Find this quiet time daily and spend time not just talking but listening.
- Stop your mind and be still in your thoughts. Listen to what is being communicated.
- Keep it up! Don't give up or get discouraged, there are varying levels of maturity in relationships so it's unreasonable to think the relationship is well-oiled when you first start.

Once I gave up control, my life started to exhibit control. I'm not suited to be in the driver's seat, but I make an excellent passenger! Get in the passenger seat!

~~~~

- Find a higher power, something greater than yourself. Acknowledge this higher power has a broader perspective than you. It helps guide you and teaches you lessons along the way, and always has your best interest in mind.
- It's crucial to meditate regularly (daily). Don't meditate just when you need something, get quiet and be quiet enough to hear an answer.
- You will feel a weight lifted off your shoulders when you give over control. Your stress, anxiety, and overall health will improve.
- Get in the mindset that challenges in your life are intended to coach and teach you, they are life lessons to help you improve.

Chapter 5: Getting Vulnerable

As popular as vulnerability may have become after Brene' Brown's famous Netflix feature, it's 100% necessary to optimize your life. If you don't know the context, vulnerability is exposing yourself both physically and emotionally to the potential of being harmed or hurt. Although that sounds negative in nature, it's neither a positive nor negative, it's simply the root of feelings. Allowing yourself to be vulnerable will allow you to take risks, to experience love, to feel courageous, and to be empathetic. It's what you need in order to experience true connection. It's allowing yourself exposure to the outside world and allowing yourself to connect and feel, regardless of the outcome.

Vulnerability is writing this book and putting it out there for you to have a view into my life without fear of your response. You may love this book, you may disagree with me, you may judge me, and you may have a life-changing experience. But, if I don't put this book and the content out there, then I will never achieve the intended purpose for this book -- to help you and others reclaim your lives.

If I write this book at home and never publish it, then I will never know if I can impact lives through my story. That's being vulnerable -- sharing and being raw and real. It starts with my opening myself and putting it all out there. As part of setting the proper foundation as you make changes, you have to allow yourself to be vulnerable and willing to deal with whatever comes your way as a result.

Allowing myself to open up was unfamiliar territory to me. I had hid myself for so many years. Like I've mentioned before, at the age of 12, I had gone down a deadly road of an eating disorder and I had become very good at hiding what I did not want you to see. I learned deception and what to show you to believe my life was picturesque. I learned how to distract people's attention to only what I wanted them to see. I learned to be convincing and tell a compelling story. I learned to make jokes and deflect conversations if people got too close to the truth. I learned how to show you everything you wanted to see and change when you blinked. I learned how to live two distinct lives. I was able to keep my struggles and my strongholds isolated and I didn't need anyone or anything to know what was truly going on.

I wasn't a bad person, and neither are you. I just had areas of my life I acknowledged were not what I wanted them to be and I didn't want anyone to judge or see what was actually taking place. In fact, I think many people that knew me would probably have some nice things to say about me, as they were often complimentary. However, I had over two decades of mastering the art of living a double life. It became a natural habit. I was able to show people what I wanted them to see and I identified myself with the person that people got to know. My wall not only prohibited me from being vulnerable, it also limited my capacity to have truly deep and loving relationships since I had completely isolated and encapsulated an entire piece of who I was. Even I didn't want to see her.

I thought I had two worlds that did not overlap, but the further I grew into my addiction, the more I realized I was wrong. My worlds were bleeding into each other and the addict in me was clawing her way up and seeking dominance in my brain. I began isolating myself more and more, minimizing exposure to the outside world. I found that I would spend a limited amount of time with friends, only to hurry home so I could drink without any judgment. I didn't want others to see what was happening in my life so allowing them to get a glimpse of the good, before it got bad, was always the plan. What I was doing was keeping people that cared about me at bay, close enough to me to have a good time, but not close enough to really get to know me. If I wanted my double-life to end, and if I wanted true and meaningful relationships, then I was going to need to tear down my walls and get vulnerable.

When the gentleman told me I needed to learn to love myself, thoughts of loneliness circled my mind. I hated the thought that the very thing I hated was keeping me from close relationships. My addiction made me create a wall around myself and my connection to people, places and things was unachievable. I couldn't bring half myself to the table and expect that to be enough for someone, so I needed to make myself whole. It wasn't fair for me to keep anything hidden. The only way I was ever going to be able to achieve a deep and meaningful relationship with someone else was if I was able to connect with myself and I had no idea who I was. I had to take my own wall down and unwind years of pain, cover-up and shame. Yes, it all came down to loving myself, but how did I get there? I didn't want to face it at first, but I had to learn to be vulnerable.

Understand your worth- and you are worth it

In order for me to want to put myself out there, I had to understand my value. It's the law of attraction or the boomerang effect. You get what you put out. My dating was horrendous. I found men that did not value me and I equate most of that to not valuing myself. If I truly wanted to achieve a positive connection, then I had to have a positive connection with myself. I had to be vulnerable with myself and open up to allow myself to peer in and get to know me.

It's entirely possible to be going through life and not know who you are. I was there, so I can attest. I didn't want to face myself. I preferred to drink and cover up than face myself, but I had to get to know me. I needed to appreciate my value and hold myself to a higher standard, and for all of us, it starts with allowing yourself to be vulnerable with yourself.

Learn to communicate

Communication is an aspect of vulnerability. You are communicating a message and whatever you put out there, you have to be prepared for any response. Communication is done both verbally and non-verbally. We are constantly communicating a message even when we might not be aware. You need to become aware of the message you are sending and you cannot be afraid to put it out there. It's communicating how we feel, it's communicating what we want, it's communicating what we need, it's communicating what we are striving for, it's communicating what we want to achieve, it's communicating our emotions, and it's communicating our desires. This can be done in a variety of ways: our voice, our actions, our gestures, our facial expressions, social media, or even an email. Communication is not simply black and white. There are loads of ways we interact with the outside world, so start paying attention to the message you are and are not communicating. It can be vulnerable, but you need to communicate to get your message across.

Let go - don't hold back

Ever walked into a situation where you became immediately paralyzed by fear? Maybe you were about to propose to the love of your life, knowing full well that you were in love and wanted to spend your life together, but you froze. With the ring in your pocket, you started to fear she may say no, even if you wanted so badly for her to take your last name and share every waking moment together for the rest of your lives. What happened? Your confidence diminished. You started over thinking what might happen. You started to fear she would say no and then what? You know what happened? You did not allow yourself to be vulnerable. You came so close. You bought the ring, you planned the dinner, and you even asked her father, but then you feared her rejection.

Taking a leap of faith is scary. I remember when I went paragliding in Lima, Peru and the guide told me to run off the cliff. Are you crazy? This wasn't a step. This was a cliff that was thousands of feet to the bottom. What was even scarier was that I had to run off the cliff before the parachute was even in the air! Had the chute been up then I would have been less anxious about the situation, but here I was just running, hoping the parachute would go up and I would not plummet to my death. Sounds dramatic, but you try it out and let me know how you feel! As soon as I stepped off the ledge, the parachute caught wind and I was gliding along the coast. As I glided through the air, I felt weightless as my feet dangled in the air. I felt untouchable, as I saw the cars driving along the road beneath me. The wind brushed my face as I gazed in awe at the beauty of the city which I could now see from up above. It was one of the most magnificent feelings and had I pulled back, I would never have experienced the pure joy and freedom I felt.

What if you decided not to hold back and you gave that ring. What's the worst that can happen? She says no? Then what? Yes, you're hurt, but maybe you then find that you were really destined to be with someone else, or maybe you avoided a bad situation with this woman that you didn't foresee when you were wanting her to be your wife (there's that Garth Brooks song again with his 'Unanswered Prayers'!). What if she says yes? Maybe you become the happiest man on earth and you experience a joy that you have never felt. You don't know what the outcome is going to be, but if you stop yourself, then you'll never find out. Being vulnerable is putting it all out there regardless of the outcome. Whatever the result, let go, don't hold back.

Accept the outcome

Rejection can hurt. I get it. As we discussed already, we cannot let fear impact our ability to be vulnerable. If we are always afraid of rejection then we will never be able to experience some of the joys in life: love, deep friendship, and winning. Therefore, we need to accept the outcome, even if it is not what we had imagined or intended.

When I was 25, I married a man I had dated for less than a year. I had allowed myself to be vulnerable by sharing my heart and my life with this man and after a few short years, it ended. I didn't know walking into the marriage that it was going to end and it was a risk I was willing to take. I don't look back at this experience as negative, but instead it was truly a building block in my life that helped me understand relationships better. I had to accept the outcome and find the positive in it. Had I not married this man then, I would have missed out on some truly wonderful experiences in life and some very valuable lessons.

Life is not always going to go the way we expected and what we want is not always what's best for us. However, there is a much larger picture at play when we know that everything that happens works in our favor in the long run. If we get fixated on one detail and one outcome, then life will keep going, and we'll get frozen in time. Accept the outcome and move on. Shift the game plan along the way.

The power is in your actions and your response. You move forward or you don't, you get paralyzed, or you accept and move on. Move forward, accept, and move on. You're finding your power -- own it. You don't get reward without the risk. Work on opening yourself and commit to being vulnerable.

~~~~~~

- Being vulnerable will allow you to open up and experience love in your life. By doing so, you

are opening up your mind and your heart to the potential for deeper relationships.
- Don't hold yourself back from making a move, step out and move boldly.
- Move forward, accept, and move on.

Step 2: **Eliminate**

You've recognized your life isn't where you want it, and you're committed to a change. Now, you want to lay the foundation, which starts by eliminating what is weighing you down, holding you back, stealing your power, and standing in the way between you and happiness.

No builder puts up walls before the foundation is laid. What would the walls be secured to? Would you put drywall into dirt instead of laying down concrete? Would the plumbing go on the outside of the house? Foundation comes first, and then you start to build.

Even if you were able to get up bits and pieces of the house, all it takes is one storm to come barreling through and the house *will* crumble. You don't want to be that house-- you don't want to create a temporary fix. You want solid, unshatterable change that will last a lifetime, and it starts with building the right foundation. This means eliminating the things that no longer serve you.

Chapter 6: Minimize to Maximize

Minimizing material 'stuff'

At a point in my life, my ex-husband and I had a fully furnished 3-story home. We had the cabinets filled with decorative plates and serving platters. There was every type of wine glass and beer mugs you could imagine. There were clothes in every drawer. The house was everything you could want and then some. It was a comfortable first home. Although I don't think it was excessive with unnecessary items, it was filled in abundance and there were items that did not get used that collected dust.

After my divorce, I moved to California getting rid of almost everything and taking only what could fit in an SUV as I moved across the country. That same year, I moved again and wound up in Texas with even less than I had brought to California. I had stripped my life of almost everything I owned, and there I was, sleeping on a blowup mattress for almost an entire year! When I was settled in Texas, I didn't repurchase everything at once, only those items that seemed to be necessary.

I had become accustomed to the amount of 'stuff' that was in my house. There was nothing in my space I didn't use or need on a regular basis. I didn't realize how accustomed I had become to living with so little until my parents had shipped several boxes of kitchen items and other random décor to me. I remember opening the boxes with a wave of anxiety passing over me. I had lived for so long without any of these items and I was overwhelmed thinking about where I would want them in my space. Seems extreme, and I didn't expect that behavioral response, but there I was, anxious over having items in my house that I did fine without.

I remember walking down the aisles at Target thinking about those necessary items I would need in my life. What were all those things I kept under my sink to clean my house? What were those 'things' I kept in the closet? What were all those boxes in the attic? Turns out, when I went back to buy the necessities, it was a lot less than I had in my previous life. I began to look at things purposefully, and quite frankly, it was too much to move around with so much stuff. Life was just easier with less and I moved around quite a bit those next few years.

As I put away the dishes and items my parents sent me, I realized I was filling my unused cabinet space with things that did not make me happy and that I would probably never use. I had a wave of anxiety because I felt obligated to these items even though I hadn't laid eyes on them in years. After a couple of weeks of grappling with this awkward feeling about these items in my little apartment, I decided to donate the majority of them. There were, however, a few items I thought I *should* keep: china, unused silverware that went with the relatively unused china, and a handful of other items. I kept the items I felt were more monetarily valuable. Therefore, although I did not want to fill my cabinets, I ended up storing some items in case I ever wanted them in the future.

After living in Dallas for 3 years, I decided to take advantage of the rising housing market and purchase a home before I was unable to afford one. I purchased a quaint, little 100-year-old home. Since it had been quite some time since I had owned a home, I thought I should do the décor thing and make it look homey. I found that I was pretty particular about what I brought into the house. I liked the look of openness and unused space, with less things for the eyes to bounce around at. For the most part, I kept to my minimalistic lifestyle, but I did start to accumulate some things and over time I found I had introduced things into my space that were more 'nice to haves' than served a purpose.

When I started down the path of transforming my life, I had so many feelings and sensory happenings. I felt like I was swarming in my mind. At first, it seemed a bit hard to focus. I'm sure some of that was because I didn't know where to start and my mind was all over the place. What I also found was that I was distracted by things that did not bring me joy, didn't bring any value, had bad memories, and didn't serve a purpose. These came in the form of people, places and things inside and outside my home. In order to have a fresh start, I was going to need to have the proper environmental conditions to foster the proper growth. You can't plant a seed in a rock and expect it to grow. It has to be in the right soil with the right amount of water. Therefore, I started going through my physical house to get rid of the rocks impeding my growth.

I got rid of anything and everything that had a bad memory or bad vibe -- items that I didn't use (but was holding on to just in case I did) and whatever I felt didn't serve a purpose. I got instant gratification on ridding myself of these items, especially those items that had negative memories associated with them. It didn't matter how new, how old, what the item cost, and how many times the item got used. If it didn't have a purpose, good memory, or it wasn't being used then, it was gone.

Probably one of my more extreme examples during this process was my truck. Before my transformation began, I had sold my 2015 Ford diesel F-250 and traded it for a GMC. I hated every minute of it. I don't need to get truck crazy on you, but I didn't feel good about the size, the weight, the fuel, the seats, or really anything about the truck (other than the 37" tires and the lift. Oops- I said I wouldn't go truck crazy here). I literally disliked every time I got in the vehicle and started driving around (I'm not smashing on GMC, I just love Fords). When I made the commitment to surround myself with things that brought me joy, the truck was one of the first things to go, even though I had only had it for 4 months. I missed my old Ford so much, that I went and bought a similar 2015 F-250 again and lost $8,000 in the transaction. I knew it was not a wise financial decision, but honestly, I was more concerned with my happiness than anything at that point. I knew I was going to need to make radical changes and if getting my Ford back was part of that, well then, so be it. When I drove off the lot, I didn't have any anxiety. I didn't look at other Fords and question my decision to trade. I didn't hate the experience. I was comfortable, and my mind was at peace. Yes, this was a little more on the extreme side, but I'm glad I ultimately made this decision at this time. Let me point out here that I'm not advocating you go buy every toy that could bring you joy, that you should make poor financial decisions based off feelings or do anything irrational. This was my one splurge in life and I made the decision knowing it was a bit impulsive and financially irresponsible. The buck stopped there for any other large decisions or changes in my life at that time.

I assessed all the possessions in my space and whatever didn't cause me to be happy, whatever didn't have good memories, and whatever didn't have a positive vibe or had a purpose, was out! It's literally as simple as that!

My folks (completely unaware of the transformation I was undergoing) came to visit me shortly after I began on my journey. I took this as a perfect opportunity to have my mother help me go through all my necklaces to see what I wanted to donate. Over the years, I had accumulated more necklaces than I would ever wear, and I systematically hung them on an organizer on the back of a door. Somehow, some of this jewelry had managed to stay with me for a couple of decades. Some had gone entirely unused. I suppose I could rationalize them since they didn't take up much space. Most of them had a memory tied to them, which is probably why I would keep them, but I never actually wore them.

Though the necklaces hung on an organizer, they were piled on top of each other and constantly tangled. It was a constant battle to not just find the necklace I wanted to wear, but also to get the necklace untangled from the rest. For years, this seemed acceptable, and I spent gobs of time and frustration to get the right necklace for the outfit I was wearing. Now that I was simplifying my life, I no longer wanted the constant battle of untangling necklaces I would never wear blocking me from the few pieces I really enjoyed.

I laid out all of the jewelry on the bed and about 90% I decided to donate. I didn't take any time in making the decision and quite frankly I didn't need to elicit any advice or opinion from my mother. If I didn't envision me wearing it in the next two months, then I got rid of it. If it had a bad memory, then I got rid of it. If I just downright didn't like it, I got rid of it. I probably went through 100 pieces of jewelry and was left with only a handful. I put all my items in a large bag and then in my closet, to donate to the women's shelter.

The next time I went to get a necklace, I realized how this one little modification made such a big impact on my day. I introduced unnecessary anxiety into my life by having too many choices and a tangled mess I had to address each time I went to grab a piece of jewelry.

After the massive purge, I had roughly 10 choices and none of them were tangled. I could see all my options without having to move things around. It had become a rather enjoyable experience, in all honesty. I took out the frustration and simplified my life. It was a small win, but you have enough of these obnoxious and frustrating events that they'll weigh you down and you won't even see it coming. I saved time and frustration, allowing me to focus on far more important things in my life than what necklace to wear.

Things are easier - what about people?

It's not just decluttering and minimizing what is in your home, you also need to assess who is in your immediate circle. People have a major impact and influence on your life so you need to be fully conscientious of that impact, big or small.

When dealing with people it is not as easy as throwing out an old pair of shoes and I get that. In order to create an environment where you are able to grow and thrive, you need to know who could be promoting negativity, encouraging or enabling your behaviors, and weighing you down.

Think about who you are interacting with on a day-to-day, who you text with, who you spend your time with, and who you call on the phone. Think about the type of communications you are having. Are they positive, are you being built up to be your best self, are you encouraging each other to do better, do you feel happy when you're around them, and do they serve a positive purpose? OR, do you find your conversations negative in nature, are you constantly gossiping, are you anxious, do they enable you to be less than the potential you know you can achieve, do they encourage the behaviors you want to eliminate, or do you find that you are seeking their companionship more so than they are seeking yours? If you find that you have people that fall into the latter category, then you need to make a hard decision if you need them in your life.

It's just as much for your good as it is for them. There may be a co-dependent relationship, or a breeding of negativity that needs to be broken, so it benefits you both to make the change.

It's the same for the items in your home. If you have someone that is not serving a purpose, then it's time to take a hard look at where these people fit. When I made the decision to get sober, I found I had a far fewer friends than I realized and a greater number of acquaintances. This wasn't because I lost my 'drinking buddy', this was because I saw that I was investing far more time into people than they were into me. I realized I was reaching out to people more than they were initiating any form of communication. I decided this was something I was no longer willing to do. I needed to be just as much a priority to them as I they were to me. If there was not a mutual interest in each other's lives, then I didn't need to make the effort to force myself into their life. Additionally, there were people who were spewing negativity and some who were outright toxic that I was no longer willing to put up with who needed to go.

Making changes when it comes to people can be tricky and more difficult than getting rid of an old t-shirt. I believe people fall into three distinct buckets:

1. **Better off Acquaintances:** There are people in your life who when you are around each other you seem to feed off each other's negative energy. You may even go do fun and seemingly healthy activities with this person but you find that you are constantly complaining and your conversations are negative in nature. This person might not be encouraging you to partake in whatever lifestyle you are trying to remove yourself from, but they certainly weigh down your mood. On the other hand, you may find that you have people that want to hang around you for what you have to offer and they use you. You might also find that you are way more invested in them than they are in you. These people need to be kept at a distance. I changed their names in my phone and I stopped reaching out to them. I didn't block them and I still cared for them, but I needed their energy to be directed somewhere else. It was counter for me to reach out and spend time asking how they were doing when it always was negative. I needed to focus on me. If this person contacted me, I would be cordial, but they went from friend status to acquaintance in my mind.

2. **Toxic Waste:** There are those people that are toxic to your life. Maybe they encourage you to engage in behaviors that do not uplift you, behaviors that drag you down, and behaviors that will keep you from ever achieving your goals. On the other hand, maybe they are so incredibly negative that you feel like a building just fell on you and you can't move. Maybe they are physically or verbally abusive, or they tear you down. These people need to go. I don't care if you block them or just stop hanging around them, but they are dragging you down. They aren't just 'having a bad day', they are bottom feeders and you don't need them. "But Jen, that's harsh!" Is that so? Let me tell you, if you want to keep being where you are, then keep them around. In fact, if you're looking for some encouragement to never make change and stay sucking from the bottom, keep them around and see what happens. We could be talking about life and death here -- trying to kick heroin, breaking up with alcohol, leaving an abusive relationship, or dealing with something else that may claim your life so you have to get serious (and even if it's not so life-threatening, you still won't progress forward if you keep them around). These are the types of changes you will need to make, in order to be successful so I want you to take this seriously and really assess who falls into this category and make the right changes. These people have to go!

3. **Your True Friends:** These are the people that care about you and want to help you in your time of need. These are the friends and family that are going to be there through thick and thin. These are the people you want around you. They genuinely care for your well-being and uplift you. Keep these people close. This is who you want to be around with.

What do you do when people keep coming back into your space when they are no longer wanted? Here are some suggestions and, depending on whether they fall in category 1 or 2 as listed above, this may dictate which response(s) you choose.

- Stop reaching out to them
- Decline their offers to hangout
- Give them the cold shoulder
- Don't respond to their text immediately -- give it time
- Don't respond to their text at all
- Tell them flat out that you are not interested in keeping the friendship alive
- Block them on your phone, social media, etc.
- Change their name in your phone to something that reminds you not to reach out or respond.

At some point, they're going to get the point. If you tend to avoid confrontation, the cold shoulder approach will take longer to get the point across, but they will get it at some point. Just stay firm in your stance-- it will only make you better in the long-run. Ridding yourself of negativity and toxic waste and keeping it at an arms-length will allow your space to be filled with people that will help you grow in right direction.

Please know that this is not extreme, it's necessary. This is your life and your happiness. It's not fair to you to have anything that weighs you down. It's time to be selfish about who you want in your life and who you don't, and you don't owe anyone an explanation or justification. They will get over it and so will you.

Oh but wait -- what about the place where I hang out?

You need to take a look at the physical locations of where you spend your time. Do you spend the vast majority of your time in places that are fostering positive energy? If your answer is no, then it's time to assess your location. Apply the same logic as you did for the things and the people in your life. If there are bad memories, if you are not able to be your best self, and if there is negative energy, then you need to make a change.

But Jen, I hate my job but I need to pay my bills! Do I just quit?

I'll give you a little insight into my journey. When I got sober, I decided not to make any drastic changes to my situation during my first year of sobriety. I wasn't thrilled with where I lived (was an 'up and coming' area and heard gun shots and reports of crime all around me) and my commute irritated me. I felt my potential at work was being undervalued, as was my paycheck. I was recently single and although I wanted to be in a relationship, I knew it was best I focused on me for the next year and not make any big changes.

You may assess your situation and determine that your job 100% needs to go, but let me walk you through my rationale on why I stayed with my job. Sure, there were things that irritated me and areas that needed to be improved upon, but my #1 focus needed to be on me. I knew my job, I was proficient at it. I knew the players and the processes, and had I left for a new opportunity I would have had to put in long hours, prove myself again, and learn a whole new job. I wasn't willing to take the energy away from myself and put it into a new opportunity just because it wasn't my dream job. I decided it was more important to focus on me. I could have left for more money, a better title, more responsibility, and so on, but I put my differences aside and focused on my well-being, and not the petty irritants at work.

Fast-forwarding the year, I found I actually liked my job and it was my mind that needed to change. This is precisely why it's important not to change just anything in your life, because maybe it is a change in perspective that is actually needed, not a change in your situation. Just focus on eliminating what can easily be removed that won't impact your life and what it truly toxic.

Does it apply to beliefs?

Yes. The answer is yes. You need to address what beliefs are not serving you. What are you so adamant about that is holding you back? What thoughts bring you to negative conclusions? What raises your blood pressure when you think about it? Look at these and determine what is toxic to your life. We'll address this more in structure, but start thinking now about what beliefs might be actually weighing you down.

~~~~~

Decluttering my life of things, people and places allowed me to focus on what truly brought meaning and purpose. I had freed myself of everything that reminded me of memories that I needed to let go of, and I kept only items that were positive and served a purpose. It was here that I was able to better visualize my life. I wasn't distracted with clutter. I had created an environment in my home that brought me peace and allowed me to focus on other areas of my life. It was sort of like standing naked in front of a mirror. I was now completely exposed and could see it all.

The reality is that the more we have in our life, the more complicated it gets. If you have a plethora of decorations and appliances on your counters in your kitchen, then you have more to clean around. It takes more time to dust and more things to worry about breaking, that's the fact. Find those pieces that are necessary, the ones you use, the ones you want to highlight, and keep those. If you use something once every few years, do you really need it (no, I'm not talking about Thanksgiving dishes)? If the answer is no, then maybe it's time to get rid of them.

You don't necessarily need to donate everything. In fact, I ended up selling a bunch of my things that I no longer wanted! I then, took that money and put it towards something that had meaning to me. I ended up with a killer tattoo and a couple of amazing snake jewelry pieces, and all those had meaning and purpose. You can donate or you can sell, but whatever medium you choose to get rid of your items, make sure you don't hold on to them for too long before you get them out of your space. Give yourself a few weeks and then take them down to a donation center to get rid of them. That way you aren't introducing more stress into your life (trying to coordinate selling items can be a job itself). Since I felt I had pretty nice things, I actually took some of those items and gave them to people I felt would appreciate them. I enjoyed this act of being thoughtful. I felt as though I was being a good steward to the items I had once chosen to put in my house and I was finding them a better home.

I now could really dig into different areas of my life and start to work on them. My white canvas had a few strokes. I now had rid myself of the clutter and anxiety, so that I did not lose sight of what I was trying to accomplish.

SENSORY MELTDOWN

There is such thing as a sensory meltdown, which is a reaction to sensory overload. It is sometimes mistaken for an outburst, but the difference is that sensory meltdown does not have a purpose. It is simply a result of over stimulation. This is often seen in children as they are still growing and learning to adapt in the world. In these instances where a child has a meltdown, professionals recommend removing the child from the environment and placing him or her into a calming environment with minimal stimuli. I believe that most parents that have a child suffering from sensory overload and is acting out would want to take the advice of professionals. I would imagine the goal would be to find an environment where the child would be able to calm down and find peace. This is how we need to treat our everyday lives in order to avoid being worked up or overwhelmed by all the stimuli in our lives.

When there is too much to look at, too much to feel, too much to hear, too much to keep clean, too much to manage, too many people to call, too many things to put away, too many dependencies, too many people/places/things vying for your attention, and too many responsibilities, we are suffering from a sensory overload, and we have the potential for a sensory meltdown at any age. This is anxiety, plain and simple. When we are anxious, the body releases cortisol and adrenaline, which have been linked to long-term physical conditions. Therefore, not only are we blocking ourselves from truly focusing on what matters, we are also increasing our risk of health conditions and a breakdown, if we allow too much stimulation in our daily lives.

Taking a step back in our lives and acknowledging activities that are priorities versus what are not, evaluating material items that are needed and purposeful versus what is nice to have (and it might even come down to looking at the people you surround yourself with and putting priority on who you spend your time with), will help give us focus in the big picture.

There are varying levels of degree of minimalism, but at the core, it is surrounding yourself with purpose and meaning. Being a minimalist does not mean you own nothing, it means you have purposeful things in your life. You need to look at the people, places, things and activities, then prioritize. It's okay to let things go and move on. If something does not bring you happiness and is littered with bad memories, then it's time to make a change. If you are constantly frustrated because you feel you don't have enough time for anything, then evaluate what's in your life and remove some of your activities. If you feel overwhelmed by clutter, then go through and remove anything that does not serve a purpose (if hoarding is an issue, then I highly encourage you to have someone help you through this exercise).

Minimizing and reducing the clutter in your life is liberating. You will not only free yourself of anxiety, but you will free up time and space in your life to really be able to focus on what matters. You can proactively avoid a sensory meltdown, which is good not just for you, but anyone close to you as well. With your new-found liberty, you will find that you are now more free to focus on you! Time and space are no longer luxuries. They are realities.

As you go through your life and assess the people, places, things and beliefs that are cluttering your life, you need to be assertive in how you prioritize what changes you are going to make. If something is truly toxic, then this should take priority of being removed. If it is easily removable with little to no impact on your life, then get rid of it. Whatever falls in the middle should be addressed at a later stage. This time of change should be focused on you, so anything that is going to detract from that should be put on the backburner. What you may find, is that these things in the middle may not be as bad as you imagined them to be and maybe it was a hard reset on your life that you needed in order to really appreciate them.

~~~~~

- Focus on people, places, things, and beliefs that can easily be removed or are toxic to your life.
- This is your time to eliminate unnecessary items, which includes negativity.
- Minimizing will allow more clarity on what is purposeful in your life.
- Identifying what serves a purpose will help give you a deeper appreciation for what you do allow in your life.
- Positivity will start to shine through once the negativity, toxicity and clutter is removed.
- Minimizing will reduce anxiety from sensory overload, which will improve mental health.
- Big changes should be assessed carefully, as this is your time to focus on you, not create havoc that could make things more difficult.

Chapter 7: Anger- Removing the Root of all Evil

Anger has been linked to health issues, crime, physical and mental abuse, among a host of other negative effects. Even though I was aware of the consequences, I never stopped to think about my own anger and the harm I was doing to me. What I came to realize as I became more self-aware was that I had a shocking amount of anger. When I tell people that addressing my anger was one of my first steps, people were generally surprised. I appeared relatively happy, so it didn't compute to people that knew me. It was one more area of my life I had kept hidden. On the outside, I appeared to be a pretty happy person! I love to smile and I love my smile! I would always tell people that if I was not smiling, that's how you would know there was a problem. So how could someone smile so much yet harbor so much anger?

Easy and I bet more of us are guilty than we realize.

It hit me that I had an anger problem one day when I was driving on a single lane toll road and a gentleman was riding way too close to my bumper. I was frustrated that he had the audacity to ride so closely behind me when I was driving the speed limit. With my anxiety rising, I reacted by slowing down to an unreasonably slow speed limit. Given we were on a single lane road with concrete barriers on either side of us, he had no way to get around my massive vehicle. I made eye-contact with the man in my side-view mirror and I flipped him off as I grinned. This was reciprocated by his middle finger and a raging man staring back at me. This seemed to go on for a couple of minutes and my blood pressure was through the roof. We were staring at each other, making obscene gestures, crawling along, since I would not only appease the man by driving fast, but I was adamant about doing the exact opposite to teach him a lesson for being a jerk and tailing me. When the road finally opened up to two lanes, we screamed at each other as he whizzed past me. I felt like I could put my fist through a brick wall. I was so mad. Reflecting on this situation, it could have ended much worse than it did. I had completely irritated this man driving behind me, and all he had to do was rear end me and we both could have wound up hurt. At the time, none of this went through my head. I was simply pissed off he was driving too close to me.

I kept thinking about the situation for a good hour and I was livid. I couldn't think of anything else, only the rage I felt for that situation. What a way to live. I allowed this man's driving to completely derail my day, take over my thoughts, raise my blood pressure, and make me think and say evil things! And for what? Literally, think about it -- what did I gain from that situation? Zero. I lost time, energy, and probably brain cells. Who knows, but I gained nothing from all that rage.

I knew I had reacted poorly, and it wasn't the first time I had a reaction like this. It seemed that over time, my escalation in these situations only kept rising, and I was probably a good candidate for something egregious happening due to my road rage. I loathed when I got this way. It usually made me shake. I would get so worked up and I could always feel my heart beating in my chest all too quickly. This is why I decided it was one of the first areas I needed to address-- it was too rampant in my life and it stayed with me far too long after every incident. I knew it existed, but I had no idea just how much anger I was carrying until I made the decision to address it. I also didn't realize just how much it was weighing me down until I was liberated from it.

Again, if you had asked me if I was generally an angry person, I would have said no. I guess I thought of Scrooge or someone that frowns and is grumpy all the time, kicking rocks around and throwing things, and that certainly wasn't me. As I began to consciously think about my anger, I could isolate two distinct areas of my life that caused my blood pressure to rise, and two situations that were unavoidable in my world: driving and work.

Companies are moving to Dallas in droves, and with that comes more people, and with that, creates even *more* traffic. Those people come from all around the country and the globe, and they all have their own idea of how driving should be. A combination of different rules of the road, too many people, not enough space, time schedules that need to be kept, accidents that are bound to happen, traffic lights that always seem to be out, trains that stop traffic forever, and all of the other factors, make driving an absolute nightmare!

I found myself constantly angry as soon as I pulled out of my driveway. I would have a running commentary at the other drivers on the road, usually the entire time I was behind the wheel. I would spew off some of the vilest things at people, simply because I didn't like the way they drove. These were all things I would never say to anyone, and I really didn't mean what I was saying, yet, for some reason, I deemed it was acceptable just because there was a pane of glass separating me and my poor victims of verbal assault.

My average day was to drive into work, spend my drive being angry, and then head into the office to smile at my coworkers, get worked up internally about something at work, smile some more and make small-talk. Then I would head back to my truck and get angry again on my ride home.

There's that yo-yo again!

I tried to keep it where no one saw the anger. I actually didn't identify myself with being an angry person! Here again, I had a double-life I was keeping hidden, but this one was not as obvious to me as my addictions.

What I came to realize was the culmination of all these instances built up like plaque in my body and I was clogged. I had become completely toxic internally. When I really took a step back and assessed my thoughts, I was more negative than positive. I spent more time focusing on the negative than thinking about the positive. All this did was cause me anxiety. We all know how nasty anxiety can be. It's the root of many diseases and health issues. The anger was causing me to stay sick in my mind and although I had no idea the power it had over me, it needed to be removed in order for me to have a healthy mind and body.

Before I go on about how I started to work on it, let me spend a moment and tell you what I observed when I watched anger in motion in my life. In addition to the racing heartbeat and the out of control feeling that I would get when I got angry, I turned to self-destructive behavior. I used the anger as an excuse to justify my actions (but since you've committed to no more excuses, this no longer applies). Maybe I needed a drink to 'cool-off', maybe I needed a cigarette to 'calm down', or whatever else that was self-harming in order to separate me from the situation.

Did I really allow these external situations to impact my life where I was engaging in self-harm just to diffuse a situation? When I look at that on paper, it makes me feel powerless. I actually gave people and situations power to get me angry, and that anger I used to justify hurting myself. That's wild. When did I give up that power over myself and when did I give it over to anything else? Could it be that a part of me snatched up the opportunity to be angry so I could justify my addictions and other actions?

So how do you begin to even start down the path of assessing your life? First, acknowledging. Then, identify when it was happening.

I was in hot yoga one night and during the cool down, I told myself that I could not leave until I had a trigger word to think of every time I started to get angry. I laid there for several minutes and thought of what would bring me instantaneous joy. What one word could I say that would give me happy thoughts? My best friend had recently told me she was pregnant and there it was. That unborn gem of a human was going to be the name I said every time I felt myself getting angry. I was committed to Riley and little did he know he was committed to me.

I was shocked. I don't mean a little shocked-- I was completely stunned over the next weeks. I said this little boy's name a thousand times. I had zero level of awareness of how many times my blood pressure would rise throughout the day. I was embarrassed with myself and how I was handling life. I never identified myself with someone that was angry, and here I was saying Riley's name every hour! After a few weeks of this exercise, there was no way I would have put myself in a category close to happiness. My thoughts were littered with negativity. I had poison throughout my soul.

That trigger word was one of the best moves I made. It made me aware of my situation, it helped to calm me, and it helped me to identify areas to work on. I got creative on how I would say the little boy's name and sometimes I made it into a song, so I really had to concentrate on removing myself from the situation and switch gears entirely.

It was good to be aware of what made me angry and it was good to be joyful thinking about the birth of my best friend's baby, but there was much more I needed to do than just identify my anger. I needed to remove the urge to get angered in the first place. Since it appeared my brain was constantly going to a dark place and negative thinking patterns, I needed to condition my brain to think positively.

Once I started to acknowledge the onset of the anger, I then started to reflect on what was making me angry. It sounds trivial and I hate to admit these, but I'm going to, only because I am sure at least one of these resonates with you. Here is a small list of the items in my day-to-day activities that would make me angry:

- I would get angry (judgmental) when I saw someone driving a hooptie vehicle that was falling apart and spitting out black smoke
- I would get angry (judgmental) when people would stop on the trail I was running on and not notice they stopped right in front of me, which would cause me to move
- I would get angry about being single/alone
- I would get angry (judgmental) when I saw someone that was homeless with an animal
- I would get angry (judgmental) when someone couldn't park straight
- I would get angry when someone parked in the spot I liked to park in at work
- I would get angry (judgmental) when someone seemed to be disengaged when they should have been present
- The list goes on and on and on and on...

This was eye-opening for me. These are trivial things we encounter all the time. Petty things that shouldn't have any impact on my life and yet, I allowed them to take precedence in my brain. I had a problem. My brain was on its own wavelength and I needed to reel the ship back to port. Here, I began rewiring the way my brain thought about these everyday interactions and situations. There were two very important practices I found that worked to alter how I viewed the world:

1. I said the Serenity Prayer until I really understood it:

God, grant me the serenity to accept the things I cannot change, the courage to change the things I can, and the wisdom to know the difference.

Accept the things I cannot change -- that's the key mindset

right there. What I realized was I was trying to control situations in my mind. When situations didn't go the way I would have imagined them panning out then I would get angry. I was literally judging and controlling so much I came in contact with, all things I had no control over! I think judging and getting angry can almost be used synonymously, as I would often judge the situation and I would find myself exhibiting some level of anger.

I then started to focus on what I really had control over (what I could change) and I mapped those against each of the items I would find myself getting angry over.

- I would get angry (judgmental) when I saw someone driving a hooptie vehicle that was falling apart and spitting out black smoke
  - Jen, you don't control what vehicles people choose!
- I would get angry (judgmental) when people would stop on the trail I was running on, and not notice they stopped right in front of me, which would cause me to move
  - Jen, you don't control when other people walk or don't!
- I would get angry about being single/alone
  - Jen, you can't control when two people will find themselves compatible!
- I would get angry (judgmental) when I saw someone that was homeless with an animal
  - Jen, you don't control if people can have a pet!
- I would get angry (judgmental) when someone couldn't park straight
  - Jen, you don't control how someone parks!
- I would get angry when someone parked in the spot I liked to park in at work
  - Jen, you are not a parking attendant- you don't control where people can and cannot park! And you don't have a reserved spot!

- I would get angry (judgmental) when someone seemed to be disengaged when they should have been present
  - Jen, you cannot control what is on someone's mind!

When you saw the list at first, quite possibly some of those items resonated with you about getting angry or annoyed. After looking at each item and what we actually have control over in those situations, it was effectively none! Was I trying to do some Jedi Knight mind-trick and control the universe with my mind? That's completely absurd! But, until I started to get a handle on my anger, this was a normal way for me to think.

2. I then made myself rethink each situation in a positive way.

I would literally think about each situation and turn it around from my original thought. Yes, this took time, but I was reprogramming my brain, so I needed to go through the exercise. I took each one of those situations (which I already figured out that I do not control), and I flipped them around into something more positive or find this behavior in my own self.

- I would get angry (judgmental) when I saw someone driving a hooptie vehicle that was falling apart and spitting out black smoke
  - Jen, this person may have been riding the bus, saved all their money and is so grateful to be able to drive himself around. It may be his pride and joy, who are you to think otherwise?
- I would get angry (judgmental) when people would stop on the trail I was running on and not notice they stopped

right in front of me which would cause me to move

- o Jen, maybe this person forgot something and bonus -- you get extra steps and you keep sharp on your reaction time
- I would get angry about being single/alone
  - o Jen, you have all the freedom in the world to do whatever you want! Enjoy the time you are single and free! Some of your non-single friends are jealous so enjoy it!
- I would get angry (judgmental) when I saw someone that was homeless with an animal
  - o Jen, this person is all alone and needs a companion. It may be the only thing that keeps this person going. This person may be someone that impacts your life one day, so don't judge them for having a dog
- I would get angry (judgmental) when someone couldn't park straight
  - o Jen, you don't always park straight!
- I would get angry when someone parked in the spot I liked to park in at work
  - o Jen, there is no assigned parking at work. If this person gets there before you, then they have every right to park there
- I would get angry (judgmental) when someone seemed to be disengaged when they should have been present
  - o Jen, maybe this person is dealing with something really

heavy outside of work that is impacting their ability to be present. It could be health, family, or friends. You just don't know what people may be dealing with.

I went through this exercise over and over, and over. It's like trying to get back in shape. You can go to the gym and look around, but you won't get the results you want. You have to get in there and do work. AND, you can't just workout once and see a transformation. You have to keep at it until you have achieved the results you want. Once you get the muscle memory, once you hit your desired weight, then it becomes maintenance but until you get to steady-state, you need to put in the work. I had to be cognizant at all times of what I could and could not control, and I needed to reframe any judgment or times I would get angry. I couldn't do this when I remembered to do it. I needed to do it all of the time.

It became somewhat of a game, a creative outlet for me. Before, I would get anxious from being judgmental and now I was creating inspiring stories behind each person, place or thing.

It took several weeks to really start to see a difference in my way of thinking, but staying committed to my own transformation started to pay off. I started to feel exponentially better. I felt as though I was starting to float to the surface of the ocean, instead of being weighted down on the bottom.

After enough practice, the muscle memory kicked in and I didn't need to be constantly making up happy stories in my head to justify people's behavior. They just stopped bothering me. It took a couple of months to hit a stride, and then I had to be aware of my actions and mindset to make sure I wasn't slipping back into my old ways.

James 1:20 states 'Human anger does not produce the righteousness of God'. Albeit religious or not, this simply states that we were not intended to be angry. Anger diminishes our integrity, pushes people away, causes disease, and causes anxiety. Reactions to anger come off strong and negatively. It can cause harm. And the list goes on. We were not intended to have anger and this is why we need to reframe our brain if we are not conditioned to think positively.

Becoming aware of what I was allowing to make me angry was first of all, eye opening, and then it was liberating. I stopped allowing people, places and things steal my joy and I took my power back.

I could see that my perspective on life had changed and I know others around me were seeing it too. The conversations had a different feel. They were light, they were positive, and they were joyful. Yes, I still had times where something would irritate me, but I had definitely made a change in my life and it was not just evident to me, but to those around me as well. I remember talking to someone about this property I had recently purchased that had been nothing short of an expensive endeavor with a lot of situations I needed to get sorted with the county. It wasn't an optimal situation for me, as I had walked into every land mine that someone could walk into. Instead of talking about all the headache, I remember talking about all the lessons I was learning. At the end of our talk, I'll never forget he said, "Woman, I wish I had your rose-colored glasses!" When I heard this, my soul became warm. I wasn't forcing the positivity, I was being truthful. Before my eyes, I had transformed the way I viewed the world and how I communicated with people.

Being told I had on rose-colored glasses was one of the biggest compliments that could have been paid to me. It showed me that my hard work of reframing was paying off. I want to say it again, I actually believed in everything I was saying. There was nothing false about what I was communicating because by then, I was in maintenance mode.

~~~~

- Anger is an anchor that keeps you from happiness and controls you.
- You give up your power when you allow yourself to get angry and empower the situation.
- Anger negatively impacts mental health and adds distractions to your life.
- Find a trigger word that makes you happy. Use it when your blood pressure rises.
- When you identify your anger rising, reframe the situation with a positive justification for the anger.
- Memorize and say the Serenity Prayer until you understand it.

Chapter 8: Power of Positivity

The law of attraction states that like attracts like: negativity attracts negativity, positivity attracts positivity. What you put out in the world, you will get back. Simply stated, the law of attraction is like a boomerang.

As my frustration and negativity became more deep-seated within me, my life and circumstances begin to spiral further. I never saw my rock bottoms while I had a positive spirit. I was always hurting with anger and frustration when I was at my lowest. I hated this person and I didn't want anyone to know the evil forces I battled internally. There I was, with two different lives again. Albeit hiding an eating disorder, hiding my drinking, hiding my anger and negativity -- I was always hiding something. I would look in the mirror and not recognize the person staring back at me because I never aligned with this monster I was hiding, but she existed. She made me ugly and that's all I could see.

I was embarrassed to let people see the person I had

become and as much as I thought my 'other life' was in hiding, the demon and ugly side of me was gunning for full dominance and she would step over the line any chance she got.

I was able to keep a façade, but the truth was that I was only sinking further and further into a depression before everyone's eyes, even my own. I felt like Fiona from Shrek -- by night one way, by day another, and I was terrified of the night Jen.

Although I kept a relatively active social life, I found myself becoming more of a recluse and wanting to spend more time at home. There's nothing wrong with being a homebody and wanting to spend time in your own space. But if your primary goal that keeps you secluded is to hide your issues, or you're too afraid of yourself, or you find yourself constantly giving in to your depressive thoughts, then there is a problem. I blinked my eyes and the once positive girl was now hiding in her house afraid of what she was capable of and who she had become.

I was dying-- my body, my soul, and my spirit died a little more every day.

Did an unfamiliar life sneak up on you and take a hold of your behavior, your attitude, and your demeanor too? I didn't actively seek to go down that road of depression, self-hate and destruction. I literally stared into the mirror at an unfamiliar face and asked how it happened.

This slow creep of negativity had taken hold of my life. I wanted so desperately to find that happy person again. I had become a prisoner in my own body. Moreover, as much as I tried to hide it, I couldn't because it was the energy that was living inside of me that kept attracting other negative energy. I may have been able to keep some semblance of positivity around me, but it became clear in a few ways that the negative energy forces had set up camp in my life.

    1. **Challenges**: I seemed to be plagued by constant challenges. It was easy for me to pinpoint the things that were going wrong in

my life and they seemed to keep piling and piling. I felt as though I was constantly wronged and wondered why nothing appeared to ever go my way. I always felt like I had the weight of the world on my shoulders. Little did I know, my higher power was trying to get my attention by teaching me lessons through these challenges, but I was wasn't receptive to learning from them.

2. **Dating**: It was clear from most of the dating relationships that I attracted other negative energies (I'll stress most, but it wasn't all). I continued to find men that had just as many issues as I did, if not more. I constantly wondered how I could keep finding these men that had so much work they needed, and the answer was easy -- my energy. I emitted energy that said I didn't respect myself and I didn't care how I was treated. I attracted addicts, narcissists and abusers. This happened one after another, after another (not all, but most).

There was clearly a strong force around me that kept finding like-for-like situations. As I took a step back and assessed the boomerang effect that was happening, it was clear that I was getting back what I was putting out. I was the common denominator in all of these situations. In order for me to achieve the change I wanted and needed, I had to work on me and I had to change that energy.

I believe it's important to understand the attraction component of energy because it's more than just trying not to be negative. It's about not attracting those people and situations into your life. You very well may need to force a smile on your face until it becomes natural. You may need to force yourself to be positive and push out that energy, and at some point, you will start to believe it and it will become you!

Emit positive energy:

1. Smile
2. Give compliments to others
3. Ask a random person how their day is going
4. Wear brighter colors
5. Stand up straight- shoulders back (shows off confidence)
6. Be engaged and focused when you talk with people, make them feel they have all your attention
7. Make yourself available to people if they want to talk
8. Call or text someone to ask how they are doing
9. Hold the door for someone
10. Give a stranger a compliment
11. Look at challenges as learning experiences and character development
12. Oh, and did I mention to smile?

These are all very reasonable and attainable goals to set for yourself that really don't require much, other than some heightened awareness of your surrounding and how you interact with them. I challenge you to focus on just 3-5 items for the next week and pay close attention to people's reactions. See if your compliment made someone smile and assess how you feel when you're engaged with the world at a more positive level. Did you notice more positivity coming back at you (that could be in a simple form of a smile)?

On the flip side, watch the behaviors and circumstances that may come off as negative and avoid those behaviors or remove yourself from the situation:

1. Avoid negative words: don't, not, can't, won't (I tell my staff this all the time to avoid these words in emails—they don't translate well)

2. Catch yourself when you are about to say a negative thought and keep it to yourself
3. Stop complaining! (I want you to reframe each one of those thoughts into something positive)
4. Stop moping
5. Avoid gossiping
6. Stop taking situations and comments personally!
7. Stop allowing fear to dictate your next move (you'll probably be amazed at the opportunities that will present themselves once you do)
8. Don't entertain negative conversations- remove yourself from them (this may even mean distancing yourself from people in your daily life)
9. Stop controlling situations. Let them play out
10. Turn that frown upside down! (Wow- I just became my mother!)

The principle of energy goes hand-in-hand with positivity but it's more than just thinking positive. It's how we present ourselves to the world and the positive energy we put out. Your focus needs to be to first identify and then to act. Simply stated, you need to identify the negative and replace those with positive and have those reflected by your actions. Once you do, believe me, people will notice.

Why is a smile harder than a frown? We have to use muscles in our face to make a smile. Therefore, naturally it is easier for us to frown (or keep a straight face), which does not give off positive energy. As we discussed, muscle memory is repeatedly doing a task, which over time, will reduce the amount of attention you need to put into completing the task because it has been committed to memory. Think of driving. Have you ever gone somewhere and didn't remember the drive? Your body is on auto-pilot and has the activity of driving committed to memory, therefore it didn't require the same level of awareness and attention as when you first got your driver's license. We want positivity to be a part of our muscle memory, where it goes on auto-pilot and it's not something we need to think about -- we just do. The muscles in our face remember to face upwards. We naturally grab the door for someone, we automatically ask how someone's day is going, and we reduce (or hopefully remove) all the negative statements we feel compelled to say.

I had become so accustomed to thinking negatively that when I looked around all I didn't notice the comparable energy around me. When I started to change my mindset, I not only began to project positivity, but I could feel the energy at a cellular level. I was now able to decipher between the old negative energy and a heightened energetic force. I became, in a sense, less tolerable of the negative energy, but also in a way more understanding. I could keep it at a distance, but I also felt more compassion for those going through their own pain. This actually made me want to be more kind to people, as I now had empathy for them and not anger. The more positive I felt, the more I wanted it. Isn't this what we are all striving for in life? It's addicting!

You know, the funny thing is that my life and my situation didn't change in the year that my brain was reframed. I still had the same job, same house, I wasn't dating, wasn't married, still had no kids, and still had no close family in Texas-- nothing really had changed in my circumstance. However, everything had changed in my brain. Whereas I once saw all of these as downers in my life, I used the positivity method to change the way I thought about each situation. As a result, I found that my energy began to change as well. I thought positively and I emitted positive energy.

I still faced challenges in my life, but I looked at those in a more positive way. My trials and challenges were teaching me life lessons and strengthening me as a human being. I wasn't the victim, I was a challenger in the game and I was set on winning. I didn't 'woe is me' all the time. I said, "Deal with it," and "Move on." I started to view what was happening around me as opportunities to learn and to grow, making me stronger and more well-rounded. I couldn't explain why everything was happening, but I certainly didn't place myself as the victim anymore. I chose to accept that things happen for a reason and many times those reasons are not always evident. I stopped trying to control the situation and started to focus my attention on how I could learn and grow from the experience.

My dating life probably exemplified the change in the law of attraction in my life. Some of the men that had once been welcomed into my life would reach out from time to time and they would quickly turn away once they saw the changes that had transpired in my life. I was always amicable, as I said. I became rather empathetic to people that were struggling themselves. As soon as I made it known that I had made changes in my life, there was almost an immediate polarization. I would say I was sober, I would say I was happy, I would say I was free, and every time they'd go away. There were many examples of energies attracting and diverging in my life, but it seemed my love life exemplified the law of attraction.

I also noticed the new people coming into my life were very different from before. These were people that believed in themselves and wanted happiness as well. Through this process, before I knew it, I had polarized people that would drag me down and put myself into a playing field with the type of companionship that I deserved.

You will see an amazing change once you start to really identify what is negative and what is positive, and then focus on projecting the right kind of energy. The positivity you are putting out into the world will come back to you. You will find that because you give a smile, you will get a smile. You will find that you get a compliment because you gave a compliment. You will find that you are surrounded by more people that want what you want -- to be happy. It's undeniable that happiness and positivity go hand-in-hand. You don't typically come across people that mope around, who also tell everyone how wonderful life is. No. These people usually have something to complain about. It's entirely up to you if your glass if half full or half empty but when I hit RESET on my life, I found that I could not progress forward if I was focusing on the bottom half of the glass. Focus on the energy you want to attract, it needs to start with you.

~~~~

- Like attracts like, meaning positive energy attracts positive energy. Focus on emitting the energy you want back.
- You can impact the energies of your surroundings.
- Your health and overall happiness will improve when you are positive.

Chapter 9: Letting go

Many of us hold on to the past and it to haunts us daily.
There are many similarities and overlaps with the chapter on
a higher power and minimizing, all focus on removing the
power that a situation, person, place or thing has over you.

The act of letting go is certainly easy to say but getting in the
mindset and practicing takes concerted effort. You may have
been harmed, abused, wronged, teased, belittled,
embarrassed, ignored, thrown under a bus, wrongfully
accused, or a thousand other things have been against you.
How can you let go when someone wronged you so badly?
How can you just let it roll off your back when you feel hurt?
How can you move on when you feel like everyone is staring
at you and talking about you? Maybe it's something
someone did to you, or it might be something you did and you
just can't let go of it. There are heavy things you deal with
and a lot to manage and juggle in your life.

I constantly carried a heavy weight: anger, fear, shame, resentment and grudges. I had allowed these to take a dominant space in my brain. I was angry I had allowed my life to seemingly get out of my control through actions, thoughts and habits. I was enraged at the physical and mental abuse I endured. I was constantly fearful my worlds were going to collide and I was going to lose everything. I was frustrated. I couldn't let people get too close to me because I was afraid what they might say if they found out what was truly happening. I was easily angered at anyone who did something that didn't align with my way of thinking. These all contributed to a high level of anxiety, unnecessary time lost ruminating on them, and complete discontent with my life. I couldn't let go of anything that happened, I carried them around like a ball and chain. I allowed my mind to be consumed by memories and harbored the feelings that went along with the. I was powerless over the past.

You have probably been in a situation where either you have personally experienced or someone you know has had an outburst due to bottling up and harboring feelings. These situations usually end up disastrously and often no one was aware of internal turmoil festering inside. Then an internal combustion happens and everyone in a mile's radius is hit by the shrapnel. What a toxic, internal journey it took to get to the point of explosion, harboring ill feelings, reminiscing on the situation, raised blood pressure, the negative thoughts, the questions, the sheer torture that went along with the situation taking up space in the brain. You don't know how to diffuse the situation because you're in the fight or flight state of emotion and you can't seem to hit the diffuse button. Your sleep is impacted and you find yourself getting sick. You're distracted, your heart is racing, your mind is preoccupied, and your life is miserable because of this situation. What a terrible place to be and yet it happens, usually without warning.

What if I told you that simply learning to let go was the remedy to that entire situation and every situation that weighs you down. All of the angst and frustration could have been avoided if you were able to actually let things roll off your shoulders. Think of how your quality of life will improve if you're able to master letting go of all those big and little things that we hold on to.

I felt like I was wearing double sided tape. I was constantly picking up lint and crud along my day-- the commute, the panic in my mind, the situations I would deal with. By the end of the day, I was covered in filth but I wasn't aware of the baggage I was accumulating. It just adhered itself to my tape and I kept going.

But how do you let go? It starts with a cognitive decision to not allow something to take over your mind. I had never consciously said I wanted to ruminate on negative situations, or that I was going to allow them to steal my joy, to affect my health, to keep me up at night and yet they did. When you are not self-reflecting and actively seeking to strengthen your mind and control your thoughts, then you risk negativity coming in and taking over your thoughts and emotions. It takes the awareness and decision to let go of situations that hold you back from living and when you let go, you'll be able to grow.

Stop controlling what you do not control:

Let's use the disastrous property I bought as an example. I applied both of the principles we discussed in working on anger -- thinking about the positive in the seemingly negative situation and identifying what I could control. With those as a foundation, I now needed to make sure I was not harboring the feelings internally.

I purchased a property that had a home that was owned by a hoarder, which was full of rats and drug dealers who lived in sheds. But, I looked past the disarray and had to have a vision for this property. Reviving the house was not an option. It had been entirely destroyed by the owner's lifestyle. Anyone looking at the property would have known it needed to be rebuilt. It was in an unlivable condition. I purchased a set of housing plans and started the demo on the house. Now the fun began.

What I didn't know was that if I leveled the house, it would get rezoned industrial. This information was not disclosed at the time of the sale. What I also didn't know was that it was close enough to a flood plain and even though FEMA records indicated the property was in the clear, the local government told me this needed an expensive survey to validate. Luckily, it was not in the flood plain after all. The survey indicated I could build on the land. Seven months after buying this property, I was given authorization to build. The house I had intended to build (plans were purchased upfront) I was told I could no longer build. Net-net, there was a lot of work, time, and money that was needed in order to get this project on the right foot.

Let's look at this situation in two different ways:

> 1. I bought a property, sunk my hard-earned money into what I thought was going to be a beautiful property I could revive. In reality, it ended up being a ton of time and money and I wasted 7 months just trying to get through the cumbersome Dallas bureaucracy, to finally get back to square-one. Not to mention, I have a million other things in my life that are taking my time and money and trying to take on this endeavor was way more than I bargained for. Since I am on a single income, the burden is solely on me to pay for the property and project, and I was constantly in fear that if my job went away, I would be up a creek with this piece of land. There was no need to loop in anyone or ask for help. I'm in this world alone and I need to work through the situation I got myself into. I'm beyond frustrated at how many people have their hands out trying to get money from me right now in all areas of my life. Don't they know I have a lot going on, and again, I only have one salary to draw from? How dare they! You want me to go to your wedding, your baby shower, your birthday party, your graduation, your house warming and I guess you want me to pay for everything for those

too? Gifts for everyone, I suppose! Can't I just get a massage for myself? No, because I have other obligations. I just need this to STOP!

Before I started to really address my thoughts, and my reactions, and try to be more positive about activities in my life, I probably would have verbatim thought the above about my situation. Let's look at what happened in the above:

- I was clearly angry with the situation
- I was mad the county made me waste so much time and money
- I was frustrated that I had no support in the world, I was the only financial contributor in my life
- I was annoyed that everyone seemed to have their hand out looking for a gift for every occasion
- I wanted to do something for myself but felt like everyone else was taking that away from me

I'm grateful to say that since I was actively working on myself and reframing my mind that I avoided most of this mindset and really tried to remain positive about the situation. This was more so the way I viewed the exact same situation:

2. I bought a property, I was so grateful I had the opportunity to find this gem and be able to buy it. It was in a transitioning area and I knew I could take it from a state of disarray to something really beautiful. I realized immediately I did a lot of things backwards and I have to think there was more of a divine lesson for me buying this land. I tend to be a bit impulsive, and this taught me to slow down, and get through one hoop before the other. I found out that I had to get the property rezoned and that was a great learning experience. Then, I found out I needed to get the land surveyed to confirm it was not in a flood

plain. Both of these I got through, and I learned
so much about the system, how to get things
done, and most importantly, how I needed to get
my property on-track for building. I was amazed I
got through the rezoning. I don't think many
people are as lucky. I really put my heart and soul
into it and even had to have a face-to-face talk
with the Commissioner to let him know what my
intentions were for the land. It took about 7
months, but honestly, I needed that time. I wasn't
prepared to jump into a construction loan, as I had
so many other things happening in my life. My
friend asked me to be in her wedding, my sister
found out she was pregnant, I started my own
business-- so many amazing things were
happening in my sphere that it was kind of a
blessing in disguise that I was forced to slow
down. I am grateful that I've been able to keep up
with my bills, with my job, and honestly, having all
of these things happening at the same time would
have been too much. As a bonus, I ended up with
a roommate for a few months during this period,
which really helped me as much as it helped her.
She was in a situation that required her to move
immediately and I was in a situation where a little
extra income was a blessing. As much as I reflect
on this situation, I know that I was not in control, I
know that my higher power knows what is best for
me, and I know that He will make things happen.
Therefore, I try not to worry. I'm not always
perfect at it, but I try to remember that I'm not in
the driver's seat and that feels pretty darn good.

When I said someone mentioned my rose-colored glasses, it
was actually about this situation here. Let's see what actually
happened:

- I looked at every step positively
- I was grateful for the time I was given
  so I could focus on some other
  amazing things happening in my life

- I was grateful to have a job that paid my bills, and I was grateful I was blessed with a temporary roommate
- I was excited about the wonderful life changes that were happening to close people in my sphere
- I realized that I was not in control, which really allowed me to let go

The main difference between the two mindsets was that I had realized that I was not in control of the situation, but I was in control of my mind. I don't control the governments decisions, I don't control who falls in love and gets married, and I don't control when people have children, so why should I allow myself to get worked up over things that are entirely out of my control? I knew buying a piece of land was a big endeavor. I just didn't realize how large it was. What I realized was I had learned a whole lot through that situation, and in the end, there was a much larger strategy at hand that was allowing me to get through it all without toppling over. Jumping in and building a home would have been too much. That's why I went through the ebbs and flows of progress. It taught me a lot about myself too, which I needed as I was rebuilding myself.

Acceptance:

Accept the situation for what it is-- nothing more and nothing less. Something happens -- let it be. Don't over think, and don't let it take space in your head. Don't review it over and over. Maybe it's something you need to learn from, so in your time of meditation, think about it, learn from it, and move on. Don't continue to let whatever it is haunt you. Tell yourself, "I will not let this steal my joy."

You will often hear me tell folks in response to a situation, "do *NOT* let it steal your joy." It's the very concept of letting go. If we let it steal our joy and make us miserable, then we are holding on to it. How many times do you go home from work and continue to think about the day? You bring it up at the dinner table, you wake up in the middle of the night thinking about it, and it's the first thing you think about in the morning. Why? Why do you allow a meeting, or a person, or an action to impact your health, and even your love life? If your child came to you and a kid said a nasty comment to them on the playground, would you advise your child to cry all night, to lose out on sleep, and get angry every time he/she saw the person at school? No! This would never be the advice you would give. You want your child to be happy and as we all know, kids are cruel. The only way kids can get through those trying times of their life is to not let the other children and the awkward phases of life they're going through impact them. You're advising to let it go.

The decision starts with you and what you are willing to accept in your life. "But Jen, I didn't ask for the weight and negativity in my life!" I know you didn't, but you allowed it to happen by allowing it in without a fight. Then you kept it around in your mind. Now you know and you have to eliminate it.

I want you to ask yourself, "Is this situation worth negatively impacting my health, wealth and love?" If your answer is NO, then tell yourself you are not going to give it space in your life to harvest and grow. Don't overthink the situation, just move on.

Learn to forgive

Sometimes to let it go, you have to forgive. This didn't mean it didn't hurt or that you'll forget what happened, it's simply an act of making the conscious decision to extend forgiveness to the person or situation. I went through some dark situations and forgiving the person that bruised you from head to toe is not easy. But it's a choice. It's for your sake, not theirs. If I did not forgive this man, then I was going to hold on to the situation and I did for years. All the anger, resentment, the shame, the hurt, and the guilt stayed with me until I learned to forgive. It wasn't enough to accept it happened and to move on. I was hurt so deeply that it was necessary to forgive.

There was no other way. I can never justify the actions of that man, so in order for me to heal, I had to forgive. As my higher power once said, "Forgive them, for they know not what they do."

Forgiveness does not mean you will no longer feel. I will always remember the hurt I felt when I told people it was a boxing incident instead of being punched by my boyfriend. It still pains my heart. But, I've made peace with the situation and I've told the situation and the person (in my mind) that I will no longer allow that situation to hurt me. I forgive him for his wrongdoings toward me. I may always feel, but I have let go and will not accept the hurt, which was gifted to me through the act of forgiveness.

Give it over to your higher power

This is where you see some of the concepts begin to blend and cross over, since we already discussed turning things over to a higher power. Think of a time when you knew someone was in control of a situation, so you didn't have to worry. Maybe it was the admin at work putting a party together. Possibly it was your mother coming by to bring you medication. Maybe it was your business partner who promised he/she would drop the check off to the bank before the weekend or maybe it was your client that said they were going to pay you by the end of the week and was always good on their word.

Why didn't you worry about any of these situations?

If the admin slacked off, then the company would have had no holiday party. If your mother didn't bring you medication, then you couldn't get better. If your business partner didn't cash the check, then the bank account was going to bounce on Monday when the office rent was due. If your client didn't pay you, then you wouldn't have any money for Father's Day that weekend.

So why didn't you worry?

Easy. Trust.

You trusted that each one of these people was going to do what they committed to doing. You had no reason not to believe in them. They had always proven trustworthy, so you had faith. My higher power has delivered His promise 100% of the time. That doesn't mean that my requests were always granted. His promise may have been different than my request but I know He has my best interest in mind, and I have to give over the situation to Him to control. Doing this makes letting go easier.

However you choose to let go, make sure that becomes part of your everyday life. Don't harbor ill feelings, don't hold on to the past, don't empower the situation by allowing it to steal your joy. Give it to your higher power, forgive, accept, realize what you can and cannot control, and take back the power you gave away.

~~~~

- Letting go is a decision you choose.
- Whatever you hold on to acts like an anchor. It will keep you from where you want to be and will impact your happiness.
- Holding on to a situation will keep you living in the past.
- Letting go doesn't mean you'll forget, it means you've made the decision to move past it and not let it control you.
- You can let go through forgiveness, acceptance, and giving it over to your higher power.
- You give a situation power if you hold on to it. Letting it go empowers you.

Step 3: **Structure**

You might be surprised to hear that I mean your mind, when I'm talking about structure, but it's the biggest piece of this puzzle, because your perception creates your reality. Old habits, creeping thoughts, excuses, fears, limiting beliefs likely go through your mind every day. The average person thinks 2500-3000 thoughts per hour. Eighty percent are negative and ninety-five percent are repetitive. See why this is so important?

Now we are about to connect the dots between cleaning out your environment, assessing the people in your life, and telling yourself to be honest with yourself. It's time to unlock your power. Where was it? Remember kindergarten? Remember when you ran from house to house on Halloween in your superman cape, and you believed you could save the world? Do you remember when you put your drawing on the refrigerator, even though you colored outside of the lines? Do you remember when you asked the neighbor girl to be your girlfriend 10 times before she finally said yes? How about that time you ran around your house naked when your parents were having a dinner party? Remember the confidence and self-love you had? You had it all along! It's just that cobwebs might have taken over.

For me, it wasn't enough to uproot myself to another city and change my surroundings to get rid of those cobwebs. It wasn't enough to get rid of material things in my home. My life only began to change when I began to reframe my mind. Here is where the real results start to shine. Your foundation is set. Now buckle up -- the ride is about to take off!

Chapter 10: Getting to know YOU!

"Jen, you need to learn to love yourself." The phrase that got the gears finally moving in my head. I don't know how many times those gears should have kick-started by hitting rock bottom yet none of those times were enough to push me to really want to change. In fact, all those rock bottoms only proved that I could actually keep sinking lower even when I couldn't possibly imagine they could go any lower or life could get any worse. Sure, I said over and over that I *wanted to* change and I certainly made many attempts but I didn't put my heart and soul into seeking change until I heard those seven words.

I can still remember feeling like I got slapped in the face and I sat there ruminating on the statement. You see, I thought I did love myself, to an extent. I thought at least I kept hidden that I knew deep down that I didn't love ALL of me. I dreamt for years about writing a motivational book, about embracing my uniqueness, and how my life was enriched because of it.

If you had asked me if I loved myself, I probably would have told you YES! However, as confident as I was in embracing my height and exhibiting a high degree of conviction as I proudly wore heels in a male dominated work environment, this man was 100% right -- I was in love with a sliver of the big picture.

For years, I tried writing that motivational book on embracing my unique qualities, and although I made some good traction, for some reason, I would always find myself with writer's block. I never quite understood why because writing is a hobby of mine. Then it hit me one day as I was driving to work. I realized I couldn't write a book about loving myself when I only loved a piece of me. It was pure hypocrisy. I didn't respect myself, I didn't like who I had become, I didn't identify with the person in the mirror, I had no idea who I was, or if I was coming or going. I did love my height. I came to love it immensely! I was proud of various accomplishments I had made over time and I did come to really like and maybe even love some things about myself. Even amidst all the good, I frankly didn't identify with the person I saw in the mirror and I loathed the monster I kept hidden. It blocked me from writing every time. One day I'll share what I wrote, but it was impossible, and quite frankly a lie, to have communicated the message of self-love, given I was on the brink of internal combustion.

I committed to myself I was going to really get to know me, to love me, to respect me, and to stop cutting myself down as I had done for so many years. I was going to allow myself to peer over the wall at the person I hid from everyone and the person people knew so I could figure out what the real story was with me.

I had so desperately wanted to be in a relationship. My biological clock was ticking and I wasn't getting any younger. This man confirmed what I knew all along. Coming to the table broken and half hidden was never going to get me into a healthy relationship -- it was a wedge keeping us apart. I had thought through this before and I knew I needed to streamline my lives and be just one person I let people see. How could I think that being close to someone and remain in hiding was possible? It made me start to question all of my friendships. Was I really allowing people to get close to me or was I limiting the potential there too?

I reached the pinnacle of my depression when I was dating this gentleman and not because our relationship didn't appear to be going anywhere, but because I didn't appear to be going anywhere. I tried to hide my melancholy, but looking back, I never kept it hidden. I went back and read texts, watched the supposed 'good morning videos' I would send, and throughout it all, my dissatisfaction with my life shined through, though I didn't see it at the time. Poor guy. What I selfishly put him through because I wasn't willing to address my true issues. I wasn't hidden at all. It was oozing out of me and I had no idea. I could keep my negativity at a distance from people that interacted with me on a plutonic and/or friendship level, but it was almost impossible to have a closer, meaningful relationship with someone without exposing my true feelings. If I truly wanted the possibility of even thinking about having kids or a family before I was 40, it was time to get serious.

It was time to get to work.

I suffered from what one may call the 'not good enough' syndrome. I was never _____ enough (fill in the blanks)

- Smart enough
- Strong enough
- Pretty enough
- Rich enough
- Successful enough
- Skinny enough
- Good enough
- You name it, I wasn't enough

For so many years, I not only neglected myself, but I was also downright abusive. I was mean to myself in a way that I would never have treated anyone. It was this double standard I put on myself and didn't apply it to others. I never walked around telling people they were fat, or ugly, or weak, or not worth it. That would just be mean and rude. But, for whatever reason, I was okay with doing that to myself. I was extremely critical of myself in all areas. I don't think it's bad to encourage ourselves to do better, but that's not what I was doing. I was flat out abusive to myself.

The more you repeat thoughts and ideas, the more you start to believe them. I truly believed I was all those things I told myself. People would often compliment me and tell me things entirely contrary to what I told myself and what I believed (that I was pretty, or skinny, or had a lot going for me), but I never internalized what they were saying. I heard the words, but I didn't believe them. I deflected the compliment just like we do when someone says our hair looks nice, and rather than a sincere, "Thank you," we launch into complaining about how it gets frizzy in the heat or often becomes unruly. I had programmed my brain to believe that I was never enough, even when I was told from friends and family that I was.

I remember being on dating sites and looking at the profiles of men that appeared to have their act together and I would shy away from these guys because I thought they were too good for me. Once they knew how bad my life had become, all the baggage I carried, then they would surely leave, so why start down that road in the first place? Therefore, I often ended up finding guys that had their own set of issues and were just happy to have someone that would accept them. Goodness, what a co-dependent mess those were (not all, but some).

I found myself in some abusive and very bad dating relationships because I didn't believe I was worth anything better. I found myself with black eyes and bruises all over my body more than once. How could I have sunk so far in life to believe that I was not worthy of a healthy relationship and it was okay to accept the abusive behaviors from men? I was once a happy and healthy little girl that had ambitions for the future. Where had my life turned that it became okay to cover the bruises with make-up and hide my pain. It hurt to see pictures of me as a happy child, carefree, and without judgment of myself. The person to whom I had become was the exact opposite.

I criticized myself for everything, every decision, every attribute, every success, every failure, every line on my face -- everything. I was mean to myself, I hurt myself, I talked down to myself, and I let myself believe I was worthless. I didn't believe I was worthy of a relationship where I deserved to be treated with respect. Anyone who was good enough to treat a woman with respect wouldn't accept all my failures and my struggles, right? So, I lowered my standards not just for how I should treat myself, but also the type of behavior I would allow someone else to treat me. It was not okay to think I didn't deserve better than the physical and mental abuse I was taking, but I truly believed it. To say this was a low in my life is a bit of an understatement. My family would have been so heartbroken and surprised if they really knew how much I hurt day in and day out, but that's what I had accepted in life.

Consequently, I kept drowning my feelings in a bottle as it helped with masking the abuse I was taking, along with a lot of other things I didn't want to feel or think about. The more I neglected myself, the more I found myself getting further and further into a dark hole and less capable at having any level of real intimate relationships. I had lost my footing and my grasp on who I was, almost ceasing to exist. I had elements of myself I knew I was confident in, but for the most part, I walked around hiding the fact that I was completely lost. Every time I tried a relationship, it failed. I didn't have a good enough foundation to stand on.

How did this happen? It's simple and in hind-sight, it's as clear as day-- I didn't love myself. I didn't put myself first. I didn't treat myself with respect, plain and simple. I got exactly what I put out in the world. In order to reverse the cycle, I needed to learn to reframe my mind to be exactly what I told myself I was not: enough.

Where did I start?

I put myself on a 'discover and learn to love me program',

and I did it by dating myself. It was truly a conscious effort to get intimate with myself and try to discover who exactly I was. Think about a new dating relationship -- what do you do? You spend time together, you get to know what the other person likes, you make time for each other, you support each other, you try to do nice things for each other so they know that you care, you cook their favorite meal by surprise, you go the extra mile, and you try to connect with them on a deeper level. This is how you need to treat the exploration of getting to know yourself and learning to love that person inside of you. Date yourself! It has nothing to do with if you're in a relationship or not, it's about getting reconnected with yourself and treating you the way you would date you.

Sure, it felt forceful, like I was stuck on an island with someone with no other options. We had to learn to survive together: strengths/weaknesses, likes/dislikes, had to spend time together, to do things together, and had to genuinely get to know each other. As cheesy as it sounds, in that process, I grew to love that person. It wasn't a switch that got flipped on overnight, but it also wasn't as hard or as overwhelming as I would have thought it would be.

- I took time to really reflect on me and learn to be my best friend
  - what I liked
  - what I didn't like
  - where I wanted to be
  - my beliefs
  - what made me happy
- I had post-its of things I liked (or wanted to like) about myself by my mirror
- I wrote 'I LOVE ME' in the shower so when it fogged up it would appear
- I gave myself an 'atta-girl!' when I did something I was proud of
- I treated myself to something nice every now and then
- I listened to self-affirmation tapes as I went to sleep

As much as I hated facing myself for so many years, going through this process wasn't as overwhelming as it seemed, and candidly, there was kind of a 'honeymoon stage' I had getting to know myself. It was actually fun to discover this person. Yes, it was a little awkward and uncomfortable in the beginning, but I kept pushing forward and forcing myself to go through these steps. I knew that I needed to reframe my mind and it was going to take persistence and dedication on my part.

At some point, I stopped looking at myself as worthless and unworthy of being loved. I had become strong and confident. I loved and respected the person inside of me. I can't say all my insecurities went away as part of this process like feeling 100% comfortable in a swimsuit or wearing no makeup in public where the scars on my face would show, but even those improved!

When I started the process of changing how I viewed myself, I don't think even I knew just how bad it was until I really started to peel the layers back and address the situation. You see, it's easy to cover up and move on. We can get so piled high in layers that we've completely covered the person we once were. When I asked if you had ever looked in the mirror and not recognized who you were, or if you had wondered where the child you use to be went, or wondered where all your hopes and dreams went, did you ever stop to think that maybe, just maybe, you had covered yourself in so many layers that in order to peel it back to square one, you were going to need to stand bare naked in front of the mirror and reacquaint with yourself?

I was there and I saw a face that I knew was mine, but it was distant and cold. There were days I wore so much literal make-up to cover up dark circles and lines on my face, I think I painted a completely different human being onto my face because it certainly was not my own. I wanted so badly to be where I knew I once was or what I was capable of being, but the more I covered, the more I spiraled, and the faster and further I drifted.

Have you tried to put out a fire? Maybe all you have is a

bucket and sand, so you throw a bucket of the tiny grit on the fire and you see some of the embers go dark. You throw another bucket full, and another, and another until the fire is no longer burning. The fire slowly goes from a blazing, magnificent orange, to dull smoke. It didn't happen on the first throw, or even the second, but at some point, the fire realized it was powerless over the heavy weight it was carrying and it finally was smothered and died off.

Now, you know you can bring that fire back, but you won't do it by pouring more sand on the pile. You need the basic elements: a spark, the right environmental conditions and the wood. When you said 'enough-is-enough' you found your spark. We talked about what you need to do in order to create the right environment by minimizing your life and surrounding it with the right elements. Now, you need to uncover the wood so you can build your fire. Taking the time to hear your thoughts, understand what you like, treating yourself, supporting yourself, and taking time just for you, are all good fire-starters. They say fake it until you make it, so make that post-it note of where you want to be next and tell yourself about it every day. Tell yourself that you look good, you're worth a healthy relationship, you're worth doing something special for, you're worth a good group of individuals that uplift you and not keep you weighed down, you're an asset to society, you're loved, you're made imperfectly perfect, and you are not defined by your past. These were all concepts that I needed to grasp and believe me, it didn't happen overnight.

We have all made mistakes and many of us just piled sand on top of them to bury them alive. They still exist. We may even berate ourselves over the situation years after the fact. It's like carrying deadweight that you can't seem to free yourself from. In order to really love yourself, you need to forgive yourself of anything that you are holding on to. Write a list of everything you're holding on to, everything that you dislike about yourself, everything that causes you pain, and use the principles you learned in letting go to get rid of all that dead weight you're carrying.

I cannot harp on the principle of getting to know and love you enough because if you don't put yourself first, then everything else has free reign to take precedence in your life. This may be one of the most uncomfortable activities you have ever done and believe me, I didn't love the idea of it, but it worked. Sometimes when you want something badly enough, you have to just trust the process. Good news is it wasn't as hard or painful as I imagined it would be. Dating myself helped me to love, honor and respect the person that my parents brought into this world. I set my foundation and dove straight into the heart of what that man saw I was lacking -- love for myself.

I went from being my worst enemy to being my biggest advocate. These days, I can't tell myself enough that I CAN do it and I actually believe it! Because if you don't advocate for yourself, then who will? All those compliments that people gave me did nothing until I believed them. I was unlocking my power from within and I never knew it could be so powerful.

Get to know you and fall in love with the person your parents brought into this world. Treat you the way you would date you, set a high bar in your life for how you should be treated. You're worth it, so understand it, believe it, and hold yourself to it!

~~~~~

- Focus on getting to know you.
- Date yourself. Treat getting to know yourself just like you would any new relationship. What do you like, dislike, do something nice for yourself, buy yourself a special give, etc.
- Stop speaking negatively towards yourself, no more tearing yourself down.
- Start to support yourself, tell yourself you can.
- You will be able to do more with a 'can do' attitude rather than a 'can't do' attitude.
- You will find your relationships with others improve when you have a better relationship with yourself.

- Your happiness will shine through when you are happy on the inside.

Chapter 11: Setting Standards & Boundaries

Establishing standards will give you direction to help establish boundaries in your life. Once you understand what you are willing to accept (standard), then you can determine your response to a situation (boundary). The two are very close in concept, but think of standard as the ideology/theory, and the boundary as the practice. The old adage, "Those who stand for nothing, will fall for anything," was me.

Standards are expectations you set for yourself, whether acceptable or unacceptable. This then becomes your guiding principle that sets the framework for what you tolerate in your life and your space. Establishing clear boundaries will ensure the standards we set out for ourselves and the expectations we have are met throughout our lives, giving us reference for when new situations occur.

As an example, this is what standards and boundaries might look like in dating:

- **Standard**: Security is top priority
  - o **Boundary**: Meet only in public places
- **Standard**: No touching on the first date
  - o **Boundary**: Let this be known upfront and have this level set, before the date happens
- **Standard**: Free dates only
  - o **Boundary**: Don't agree to go on a date that costs money, recommend an idea for a free date instead

But I'm not just talking about dating. Standards need to be set in every area of your life. I had allowed my life to be overrun by dysfunction in so many areas since I didn't set up enough bumpers to keep myself from never going in the gutter, and I didn't fool proof my life from having unwanted visitors and situations in my space. Sure, I had a moral compass and was living life with some degree of standards, but not everywhere they needed to be. In my times of meditation, I sat down and really assessed all areas of my life, especially those dysfunctional areas. Had I even set a rudimentary standard of happiness and love then I don't think my life would fallen apart, because my boundaries did not focus on either goal.

As Tony Robbins said best, "If you don't set baseline standards for what you'll accept in your life, you'll find it easy to slip into behaviors and attitudes, and a quality of life that's far below what you deserve." I was most certainly living a quality of life below what I deserved because I had never cognitively created baseline standards, which meant I dealt with every situation as it arose instead of blocking it at the gate.

As I took a step back and looked at my life, I realized I was acting entirely counter to minimalism. I was allowing far too many unsolicited people, places, beliefs, habits, and thoughts into my life while I was constantly reactively removing them. Instead, I wanted to proactively keep them out. I had given leeway far too much to come into my sphere, not minding whether it had a purpose or not. All these unnecessary things would take time and energy away from areas of importance.

Until I started to go through the positivity exercise, I had no idea just how negative I was. What I started to observe was I had a lot of people in my life that were very negative in nature themselves, and this was bringing me no value to my life. This didn't mean I necessarily had to eliminate people from my life, but I did need to establish boundaries around their negativity. I told myself I was no longer willing to allow them more than a few minutes of time to vent and I wasn't going to feed into their negativity and fuel them even higher. Instead, after a couple of minutes, I would change the topic, and I would inject positivity into the situation. Some people I cut out all together and this was a case-by-case decision. I truly enjoyed some of the people in my life and I wanted to give the friendship a chance with a new set of boundaries.

Another observation I made, and I referenced before, was I had a lot of people that I would reach out to, but it was very infrequently reciprocated. This was an empty realization as I was thinking through it and I decided my standard was not to keep friendships alive if it wasn't mutual. This didn't mean I abandoned people entirely. I actually shifted how I viewed those people. Acquaintances are sporadic and you might expect they would only message infrequently. I took all of these so called 'friends' and I put them into an acquaintance category. I stopped messaging them and it felt much more natural! I was trying to force a friendship that was really an acquaintance. When I put people in the right boxes, I felt a lot better about how I viewed the relationship. It was a lot healthier for me overall.

This may sound like a funny exercise, but I want you to do it. Write down what is important to you and set those as standards in your life. Think about relationships, work, how you view life, your personal space, and think about what defines you and start to write those down. This applies to both physical and emotional areas of your life. My list started small, but at least I had a starting point that I could then apply to various situations in my life.

Some of the standards I set included:

- I am a priority
- I need to put myself first
- Negativity is out
- I am not going to dedicate my life only to one thing
- I am not willing to be more invested in a relationship than the other person
- My emotional needs matter
- I am going to be selective on friendships and keep only a few handful
- I am going to keep some element of being carefree
- God is top priority
- Physical and emotional abuse would not be tolerated
- Live a purpose-driven life
- Remain honest with myself and others
- Sleep and exercise are a priority

Now, this is not to say that some of these did not exist in my life, but I needed to conceptualize them on paper. Those were standards that I could apply to various situations that would allow me to determine the boundaries for that situation. They may look drastically different (and these are not black and white- and the response may vary).

- **Situation**: Am asked by a stranger to go to dinner at 8pm on a Tuesday
  - o **Standard**: Live a purpose driven life
  - o **Boundary**: Say no because there does not appear to be any commonalities- the dinner serves no apparent value-added
- **Situation**: Am asked by a stranger to go to dinner at 8pm on a Tuesday
  - o **Standard**: Sleep is a priority

- - **Boundary**: 8pm is too late for dinner
- **Situation**: Am asked by a stranger to go to dinner at 8pm on a Tuesday
  - **Standard**: Selective on friendships
  - **Boundary**: Say no because I have enough friends to juggle
- **Situation**: Am asked by a stranger to go to dinner at 8pm on a Tuesday
  - **Standard**: I will keep some element of being carefree
  - **Boundary**: I will agree to dinner, but we meet for an hour, and I'm in bed by 9pm

Point being, I've tied the same situation to different outcomes, and I need to assess the situations as they arise. They will not always look the same and may be different outcomes, but I have to see where they fall in the spectrum and where they add value in my life. This stranger and I may have had a great connection when we bumped into each other, so maybe it's worth being spontaneous. Maybe this person will become my new best friend, but assess your world, and don't leave just to chance.

Establishing these standards helped me grow and develop. It's like planting the seed in the ground and then letting it grow. If you never plant the seed, you will never grow anything. Once you plant a seed, you then need to make sure it has water to make it grow or it will remain a seed.

I then wrote down areas in my life where I did not feel fulfilled or areas that gave me anxiety. This was 'low hanging fruit' the easy situations to go after. If I could identify dysfunction, then it needed to be addressed.

These areas included:

- Work
- Sleep
- Dating
- Friendships

- Money
- My perception of myself

I then thought through real situations and began applying the standards and establishing boundaries.

My work/life balance went entirely off kilter -- I was a work-a-holic

I look back at my own life and what I was willing to give one of my previous companies. I gave them everything I had: time, sanity, they even chose my zip code. I was willing to go way above and beyond. I never could get out of a state of chaos, I was constantly giving more and more, and I felt like I was drinking from a fire hose every day. I didn't want that level of madness in my life, but I never pushed back otherwise.

I had allowed it to take priority over everything else in my life (this wasn't the only job). After each move, instead of focusing on settling in and creating a life for myself, I used the excuse of not knowing anyone to justify my working even longer hours. I had allowed work to take an unhealthy precedence in my life. Work had taken the position of first place in my life, above me, above my relationship with my higher power, above my family, above my friends, and above my dating life. Imagine the shock I felt when I was let go after giving a company my everything. I remember telling people that it stung more than my divorce did. Writing that down and admitting it makes me sad. Something was very misprioritized in my life for that to be a reality.

After I was laid off, I told myself that I would never again put myself through that situation again. I would no longer put a company in a position in my life where it would take my focus away from what I needed to do in my life in order to be balanced and healthy. I committed myself to working so I could live instead of living so I could work. Once I set that standard in my life, I found that my relationship with my next company was much healthier. I was able to come into the office much more refreshed and focused than when I was burning the candle at both ends. I was grateful to have a job that afforded me the opportunity to live, but I was not going to die in the office. Now, don't get me wrong, there were times I needed to go above and beyond, but I knew that was only temporary. Sometimes, we need to give the extra mile at work, but I could not have that as the norm. That needed to be the exception. With my newfound time, I was able to focus on me and stop neglecting the person I spent my every waking moment with, which ironically enough, probably made me a better employee.

I wasn't sleeping more than 4-5 hours a night

For years, I had come to accept that 4-5 hours of sleep a night was ok. I was up too late and woke up too early. I had completely ignored the fundamental principle they teach you in grade school: the importance of sleep! I was waking up early so I could use the gym before work, but studies have proven that sleep and losing weight have a correlation, so I was actually countering my objectives. Additionally, sleep allows our bodies to repair themselves and lack of sleep is linked to an increased risk of a number of diseases. Therefore, once I determined that sleep was going to be a priority and a standard, I decided I needed to give myself a bedtime and stick to it.

There I was in my mid-30s, giving myself a bedtime, which I had not had since I was a child, but it needed to happen. I had decided to make this change in the summer, which meant I found myself crawling into bed while it was still light out. What a change that was! But I stuck to it and the strangest thing started to happen. The more I slept, the more my body craved it. It was as if I put it as a priority in my mind and then my body followed suit. I went from 4, to 5, to 6, to needing 7 hours of sleep a night, and some nights, even more. Prioritizing sleep helped me set boundaries in my life, and I was then overall more refreshed throughout the day!

My dating life was a mess

As I think back on some of the men I've dated, I think about just how much time and heartache I could have saved if I had set standards for myself. I had set some relative likes and dislikes in my dating life for the types of men I liked to date, but I had not established any real level of standards or limits on what was acceptable behavior. I found that, although each relationship was unique in its own respect, there were commonalities across many of them that I didn't acknowledge at the time. All I knew was my dating life kept failing and the common denominator was me. Although arguably, it was the men that needed to change their behavior, it was I who needed to establish what would be acceptable or not from the get-go. Since we should not expect someone to change, I had to be firm in what was acceptable and unacceptable from the start.

In almost every one of my relationships, I was dating someone that put every other priority ahead of me. It did not matter what that was: alcohol, drugs, the gun range, the dog-- I was second, at best, in all of these situations. I established the standard that I was to be a priority in the life of the person I was dating, which eliminated all of these situations from ever happening again! It's funny how I never loved myself and yet I expected a man to. If I didn't love me, why should they? Well, guess what, world? Things have changed and in no way am I going to let a man love me on a level less than I deserve in a relationship. I will be prioritized!

As I reflected on some of the relationships in my life, I began putting tangible examples in place of tolerable behaviors, which I would be able to apply to other situations and behaviors if/when they arose in future relationships:

- It was not ok to only see me two hours a week and call that relationship
- It was not ok to prioritize all your other hobbies ahead of me

- It was not ok to talk down or physically harm me
- It was not ok to rarely call or message
- It was not ok to disappear for significant lengths of time
- It was ok for me to expect something nice from time-to-time
- It was ok for me to want him to show some level of affection if we were in public (like hold me by the hand)
- It was ok for me to walk away from a relationship if I felt I was second class

Looking at this list, many of these are probably obvious dos and don'ts, but because I had never set a standard, no boundaries kept these from happening. Putting these in place has allowed me to more easily identify, discuss, address and walk away if needed. If my needs were not being met or I felt as though I was in 2nd place to everything else, then I knew this was not a relationship I was willing to entertain. I know my value and he needs to as well.

I had some friendships that were not on equal playing fields

I took a hard look at my friendships and I paired down my life. I looked for commonalities across my group(s) of friends and that aided in making my decisions. It wasn't until I began to focus on setting standards and giving myself boundaries that I really started to dig much deeper on who I considered a friend and what I wanted out of my friendships.

I didn't realize just how many people were consuming my time that had a different take on the friendship than I did until I stepped back and got honest with myself. I began to see a lot more happening around me that I was unwilling to keep entertaining.

- If I was more invested in asking you about your day than you were about mine, then you became an acquaintance and I stopped messaging.
- If you seemed interested in having a friendship with me because you thought I was just a 'pretty girl' or stood a chance, I stopped messaging.
- If some of my life choices were not respected, then we didn't need to continue to be friends (going to church, quitting drinking, going to bed early, etc.).
- If I felt friends were superficial and involved in things that I did not care to associate myself with (drugs, wild parties, chasing men for money), I wasn't interested in keeping our 'friendship'.

Friends started to notice the difference. Some questioned me, but at the end of the day, the chatter died down. Once my baseline was established, then I could continue to deepen and enhance the friendships that were worth my time.

Money: I never did anything nice for myself

For years, I didn't spend any money on myself (outside of maybe the necessities and alcohol). That included clothes, hair, nails and massages. I didn't invest in myself whatsoever! I was so frugal that I found myself in a closet that was 10 years old, hair/makeup/nails/eyebrows all done by me! Although it's good to be financially conservative, it's also important to do something for your and treat yourself. I had to set a boundary with my money and my mindset and tell myself that it was ok to buy something every now and then. As comical as that may sound, try doing something for yourself and see how you feel. It doesn't have to be over the top, but a massage after a long week is well deserved sometimes and done without guilt.

I was disrespectful to myself

It almost sounds crazy that I would need a boundary with myself, but 100%, I needed to establish what acceptable and unacceptable behavior towards myself was! In the same way that I did that with dating, I also had to do that with me. I cannot tell you how many times I would look sideways in a mirror and tell myself how fat I was. I was doing this all day long, which is mind-numbing to think about. I hated being in a bathing suit. This was one of my biggest fears! I know I suffer from Body Dysmorphic Disorder (BDD), but that does not give me the right to criticize myself for how I looked (which was just fine because I was wonderfully made and very blessed). I had to set a boundary to change the behavior of critiquing and criticizing and learn to accept aspects of myself that I hated. I still continued to challenge myself and set goals for myself, but it also meant that I had to stop looking in the mirror and playing the 'I'm not good enough' game. Now as much as I want to say that I went through this exercise and it fixed my BDD and I stopped being critical of myself, that wasn't entirely the case. I was, however, able to stop being so critical, I began just accepting that me in a swimsuit, and I feared less. I began embracing other parts of me that I once had torn apart. Work in progress!

Once I was cognizant of the changes, I was more aware of the causes and effects that were taking place. I found myself to be much happier and who would have thought all of this was just by setting standards in my life that I was a priority where my boundary was that I was not allowed to engage in self-hate?

Imagine if you had set standards for yourself all this time? Certainly, they could have helped to keep some areas of your life on track. Sometimes, we don't know what boundaries we need to set until we have actually gone through a situation, at which point we then need to step back and assess the situation and where boundaries need to be established. Knowing what your standards are, what you are willing and not willing to accept, will help to define those boundaries.

This practice is not a one-and-done. We need to continue to self-reflect and assess what is working and not working. Life happens, things change, priorities change, we get older, and we have families. We need to constantly be assessing what is working and what is not working and what needs to be tweaked. You're an adult, so make the adult assessment over your life and get real with yourself to see what is working and what needs to be tweaked. If you are not in tune with yourself at this level, then you are at risk for new situations overrunning your life.

Boundaries will set standards and guidelines on what treatment you will accept and this will help you to first assess how you want to be treated, and then create barriers to ensure that you hold yourself to those provisions you put in place. Think about what is important for you and write down some fundamental standards. Then write down certain areas of your life that need some clean up. Write specific situations and write down how you envision those situations when you align those standards to those situations. Create the life you envision seeing and hold yourself and others to that.

~~~

- Boundaries and standards give you guidelines on how you will live your life and how you will be treated (even by yourself).
- Setting standards and boundaries puts you on the offense rather than the defense.
- Establishing standards and boundaries will give you time back.
- Make sure one standard you set is to put yourself as a priority. Remember, you are worth it, you are enough, and you come first.
- When you are at your best then you can be your best for others, so it's not selfish to set standards and boundaries.

Chapter 12: Step out & Speak up!

Since I'm an alpha female, this chapter may come as a surprise to almost anyone that knows me. To think that I had any trouble speaking up would probably come as a surprise, but since I was good at belittling and neglecting myself and what I needed, I was also not very good at speaking up about my feelings and expressing my needs. What I discovered was this was a fundamental element I needed to master in order to have ownership over my life and the direction it led.

A friend of mine had taken on a roommate once to help out his friend. He didn't ask for any money. He knew she had been living in her car so he assumed she didn't have much to give. He brought her in with the assumption that this would be a good environment for her to get back on her feet, find a job, and become independent. We would go on walks and he would tell me about all his expectations and hopes for this girl. It wasn't long until I could tell that my friend was questioning his decision to allow this woman, who was at first referred to as 'a friend' then quickly became 'that woman', into his home. She was unproductive while he was at work, she would go out late at night during the week, she would eat the food he bought, she had a dating life with men that appeared to have expensive cars, and so on.

Every walk we had, the friendship between him and his roommate seemed to diminish further and further, and pretty quickly, he was at a point where he wanted her out of his house. He was feeling used and disrespected in his own home.

What I kept telling him was he needed to communicate his expectations to her. I was grateful I was able to be a listening ear, but there was nothing I could do in that situation to change it-- it was between the two of them. I would ask him if he had spoken with her and time after time, he said no. All he was doing was festering inside because he had not established and communicated any boundaries.

After many months and conversations of complaints to me (saying nothing to his roommate), he finally set his expectation with his friend. This completely blindsided her. She didn't realize she wasn't meeting his expectations and felt a bit judged for not meeting whatever ideas he had in his mind for how the situation was supposed to play out. She was never a part of the planning session, so how was she to know what was being expected of her? It wasn't long after that she moved out. Had the boundaries been effectively communicated upfront, then I believe the two of them would still be friends today. The absence of communication only allowed feelings that were bottled inside to become toxic and became very ugly when he was at a crossroad. I think many of us could look at this in many of our close relationships and see just how improving the communication would be able to make it more tolerable and easier to maintain the close relationship without negative feelings.

I was much in the same way. I was afraid to say what I needed, and like my friend, I ended up getting trampled on. I didn't speak up with others, and I didn't speak up to myself-- both needed to happen. What keeps us from standing up for ourselves?

Fear

Speaking up can cause a lot of anxiety for fear of what the repercussion may be. Many of us will over think what the cause and effect will be if we communicate what we are feeling. If we felt that we would have a positive response, then it seems pretty obvious we would communicate our position. But, if we think people will shun us, will disagree with us, will talk badly about us, will start rumors about us, or will want to put up a fight with us, then sometimes the path of least resistance by saying nothing seems to present itself as the best option. Fear can paralyze our desire to communicate, which only bottles up our thoughts and feelings until they come out in the most unforeseen and negative ways like that combustion we talked about.

Conflict averse

Many people are conflict averse and would do anything to avoid it. It's not that they don't care, they just don't want to be in a situation where conflict exists. It would be better for them to be people pleasers and go with the path of least resistance in order to keep everyone happy. There are also people that believe that silence is the path of least resistance. The problem here is you ignore yourself entirely and are focused more on others than yourself.

Ever said yes to something because you didn't want to disappoint someone, even though you really didn't want to do it? Ever said yes to a wedding you didn't want to be in, or paid for a trip you didn't want to go on, or went on a date with someone you had planned on ending it with but hadn't? Think of the time, money, headache, stress you could save if you were willing to be a bit more honest, instead of avoiding conflict.

The environment does not feel conducive

I've been in plenty of situations where I am thinking something, but I just can't figure out where the place is to insert my thought/opinion. I find this used to happen in the office early on in my career. There would be a meeting with a defined agenda and the opportunity to provide feedback did not present itself. Should I wait and send my boss an email after the meeting? Should I have side-bar conversations with my colleagues after the meeting to express my concern? Do I raise my hand and disrupt the flow of the meeting? Should I write an anonymous note and drop it off in the communal 'CONCERNS' box on the admin's desk? Should I quit?

This can happen anywhere. We don't want to interrupt anyone, we want to follow protocol, we don't want to inconvenience anyone, and so we just stay shut. It's so hard to know what the best route is. The opportunity to speak your mind just does not always seem conducive, and sometimes, it's completely appropriate to cut in on the conversation and insert your thoughts.

Lack of motivation

I was honored to have been asked to participate in a special event for a friend, especially since this was while I was in recovery. To me, this signified that I was able to connect on a deeper level of friendship than I had while I was deep in my addiction, so I was elated at having been asked to participate. There were several of us that had been asked to be involved in the planning. There was a dominant woman that decided to take a primary role in the planning, which I was perfectly fine with since I had other activities to focus on. At some point, ramping up to the events, I began receiving anxious phone calls from various friends raising concern about the details they had received about the event. There was clearly a misalignment between the person planning and the people attending. I realized that although I was not responsible for making the decisions that was causing the upheaval, I was responsible for not having spoken up and setting clearer expectations in the beginning, I should have had more foresight and motivation to do so. I was focused on other areas of my life, and unfortunately, I never set the appropriate boundaries with this person that was making decisions on behalf of the group. The end result was not pretty. I had to take a stance on behalf of myself and the group which did not align with this person and she got very defensive. This lack of communication on my part ultimately resulted in our parting ways with our friendship. All this could have been avoided had we discussed what was expected upfront.

Have you ever been in an argument with someone, let's say a close loved one, and one of you was completely caught off-guard by the other person's reaction? You were going about your day, then boom, an explosion of emotions happened. Since many of us have a fight or flight reaction in these situations, neither of those options do any good to the already escalated feelings and emotions. They only add more fuel to the fire -- a fire you may not have even known existed!

Without effective communication, there is no real way to get on the same page. You cannot expect anyone to be a mind reader no matter how close you are to them. Communicating how you feel will establish those boundaries in the situation, making sure everyone is clear upfront on what is acceptable or unacceptable. It also opens up the opportunity for discussion. Don't let a lack of motivation, fear, the right conducive environment or the fact that you'd rather be conflict averse be the reason you have misaligned expectations.

~~~~

Along the same veins of communication and letting others know my thoughts, opinions and feelings, I found I had to be honest with where I was in my journey. I had committing to being honest with myself, now I needed to commit to being honest with others. It's more than just speaking up because someone has pushed a boundary, or a boundary needs to be set. It's letting your guard down and admitting where you are and what you are going through.

For me, I was pulling myself up from what felt like under the ground and I didn't just bounce on my feet over night. I took a solid year to self-reflect and really dig in and work on resetting myself into the person I wanted to be. There was no way anyone could have known the changes I was going through, the struggles I was feeling, and the challenges I faced, unless I became vocal about it. I spent so much of life covering up what I didn't want people to see and now I had to shift that entire mentality to become comfortable with admitting where I was at.

It was fairly recent after I quit drinking that I had a bachelorette trip for a friend at an all-inclusive resort in Mexico. I remember telling the bride's sister my apprehensions about going, not because I didn't want to be around alcohol, but because I didn't want to deal with all the comments I knew I would face for not drinking. Additionally, I knew I was fragile in how I felt about myself and I didn't want unsolicited comments about my age, my looks or my lifestyle. I was assured that would not happen which put me more at ease heading into the trip. Although the trip went better than expected, I still dealt with some level of unwanted commentary and got berated for not drinking. A year later, I sat with the bride and her sister, opening up more about how truly dark my life was when I was drinking. They were both shocked. They had no idea how close to destruction I was and I believe if I had been as forthcoming with where I was in resetting my life when we went on the trip (not just vocalizing what I wanted to avoid, but actually what I was going through), I would venture to bet that I would have not heard anything from any of the ladies. I can take a lot of banter. Heck, I can't dish it if I can't take it and I definitely dish it! But, because I was fragile, I knew this exceeded what I could take. Communicating with the other ladies about where I was at in my life and in my recovery, as well as what my needs were, is what I should have done, instead of being vague about what was really happening with me.

In another instance, I was invited to a friend's wedding in New Orleans. Now, for most drinkers or anyone that likes to party and get wild, this is a paradise! For me, this was an overwhelming event. I went through periods of sobriety on my road to finally eliminating alcohol all together and this trip fell on one of my many attempts to get sober. I had opened up to my friends that were getting married that I had a problem with alcohol, and while most people were out drinking-- I found myself walking a few miles out of town to a sober group meeting. I'll never forget when my friend found me later and told me just how much he appreciated me being there, knowing fully well that I was going to be surrounded by lots of temptations. His uncle was a recovered alcoholic and he was aware of all the struggles and the challenges, having watched him as he grew up. My friend could relate to what I was trying to accomplish because I had admitted to him where I was. It was actually received with a deeper appreciation for my presence, which made me almost emotional. It had been tough to be there and watch everyone partake in something I wanted but opening up freed me and allowed me to have a deeper connection with my friends.

What I found was that once people knew where I was coming from, they were better able to comprehend. There is an innate desire to want to know the why. We are very inquisitive creatures by nature. Sure, we take things at face value sometimes, but we often find that we need to know the why behind it. I know that not everyone is going to be able to relate to what I was going through. Sometimes, people won't know until they've gone through it themselves, but our minds are wired to try to understand, and sometimes, that's all we can ask of people. When we eliminate the speculations by admitting where we are at, we are bound to get a response of better understanding. It does not mean someone will always accept, embrace, or even fully comprehend, but they will have a better understanding of where you are coming from.

There was another side to opening up and communicating

my needs and feelings that wasn't as rosy. There were very distinct times I opened up and was very candid about where I was and it wasn't well received. I know that not everyone can always step up and support in the way we may need, but I felt massively let down at times when I opened up and there was nothing more than a bit of verbal sympathy.

I remember opening up to friend about the fact that I had recently been experiencing suicidal thoughts. His response was more, "I'm so sorry," and, "I had no idea,"' and that was about it. Maybe I needed to better communicate what I needed, but I felt my vulnerability was devalued and I left that friendship feeling very hurt since I thought we had a closer bond. I could have communicated better what I needed from him. How would he know if I wasn't explicit? But the fact is that not every time you open up and say what you need will it be received the way you envision. Maybe I needed to be more specific or maybe even if I had I would have received the same non-response. This is part of being vulnerable and accepting the outcome.

It's important to keep in mind that not everyone is going to know what to do with your situation if you open up for a wide variety of reasons and none of those reasons are about you. I cannot fault these individuals. It was a heavy load I was putting out there. However, through this process I realized how close, or not close, people were throughout this step in the process. Some of the friendships that I believed were close were not. I had to rearrange their friendship in my brain so I could understand the expectations from them in the future in order not to feel hurt. Again, no fault to them. I had misjudged the closeness of the friendship all along or maybe they had their own stuff they were going through that I didn't know about and purely didn't have the bandwidth to be supportive.

Fear and wanting to avoid conflict can play a big role in how we operate. We need to acknowledge that the long-term result may not outweigh the short-term benefit. We may not always know when the best time is to insert ourselves, but we do know the results. It's just like an election. If we don't vote, we don't have any influence on the outcome and no real ground to stand on if we disagree with the results. You have to get out there to vote in order to have your voice heard. Lastly, lack of motivation is an easy way out and we can't default to the easy. There is too much risk involved.

What may not be completely evident is that when we do not speak up for ourselves, we are not loving ourselves. The fears, the conflict avoidance, the environment, the lack of motivation are all taking top priority and we've decided we aren't as important. If we are not putting ourselves first then we aren't fully loving ourselves. We've used these things as excuses not to speak up. See how everything is interwoven, like I said? Every time we avoid speaking up, we are saying NO to ourselves and saying yes to being mistreated (even if it is by us). This goes back to getting to know you. If you would stick up for a friend or family member in the same situation, you should surely step out and speak up for yourself too.

Learning to speak up for myself, even as an alpha, was a critical component of my transformation. What I found was that the boundaries I set helped me in finding my voice. Not to mention, it was completely liberating not to hold back any longer! Speak your wants and needs into existence so you and others can hear!

~~~~~~

- Stepping out and speaking up helps you and others know exactly what you want and need and eliminates ambiguity and misunderstanding.
- It allows you to reach a level of satisfaction that you control vs. hoping people intuitively know what you want and need.
- It helps to liberate yourself from the anxiety of bottling up anger, frustrations, etc.
- You will learn better about yourself when you are focused on speaking your wants and needs into existence.

Chapter 13: Accepting Help

Somewhere along the way, I adopted this mentality that I shouldn't accept help from anyone. I think I had been burnt enough times when someone had done something and dangled the favor in my face that I became polarized to the idea. "Remember when I did that thing for you?!" Some of those times I hadn't even asked for a favor and yet they got turned around and became my fault or an IOU.

In one of my relationships, my significant other made the decision to get his degree. He was so proud of himself that he even told my father this was something he was committed to. I had nothing to do with this decision, other than the rest of my family is educated and everyone has at minimum of a bachelors degree. I fully supported his decision. I didn't make him go to school, I didn't force him to pay for classes, I didn't pick his schedule, I didn't make him tell my father, and I wasn't a factor in the equation. There were nights where my other half would come home after a long day of work and a class and would get completely frustrated with me. He would blame being tired on me and in anger say, "I'm doing this for you!" I never asked him to go to school, and yet this massively frustrating endeavor that was consuming his time and patience had somehow become my fault.

With enough of these situations in my past, I came to believe that anyone doing anything that resembled a favor was not anything I was interested in entertaining. I became totally independent. Whatever the task, I could do on my own.

I became adamant that I wanted to be able to support myself through thick and thin. I didn't mind helping others. In fact, I got a lot of joy from helping others, but in reverse I wanted no part of it. I never wanted to allow someone to make me feel like I owed them something for a nice gesture or a favor they did for me. I didn't want to feel like I was indebted to anyone in any way. I built this wall so high that I even pushed my parents away. It was only minimal help that I was willing to accept. I was an adult. They aren't obligated to pay for my dinner, right? I didn't want to be responsible for them ever feeling like they couldn't financially enjoy their retirement because they bought anything for me. I wanted no part of that. Even though I usually allowed them to pay for dinner, I didn't feel good about it.

I started to put this wedge in between me and those around me because I had this idea in my head that I had to do everything myself and I didn't want or need help from anyone. What I was actually doing was isolating myself with this wall I had built and neglected a fundamental component of relationships -- that people actually want to help those they care about. It's a desire to want to step in when you see a need in someone's life that you care for and I smacked down anyone that tried to reach out. Oh, and let me just say for the record that many men like someone who is independent but being too independent can yield off-putting results. Most men want to feel needed and when you are communicating through your actions that you don't need them, well, you can do the math there.

Think about the saying 'It takes a village'. We often hear that in the context of raising a child, but why does it take a village? Because we need the influence of a well-rounded community to make us well rounded. We cannot expect that a child is going to be able to get the breadth and depth of the world from just one or two persons raising them. No, it takes the influence of others to help give perspectives on other ways of life, mindsets, strengths, and so on. If we acknowledge that it takes the masses to mold someone into a well-rounded individual, then fundamentally, we are all supposed to impact and support each other. One person simply cannot be everything, yet there I was thinking I could do it all!

Looking back at this, I probably learned a lot trying to do everything on my own because I forced myself to learn via YouTube and Google for many different skills that I didn't possess, but at what expense? What did I compromise in order for me to attempt to try to do something all on my own just to satisfy my stubborn mind? I probably compromised quality, my sanity, my time, relationship building, and straight up quality of life. Oh, and I can't confirm, but it probably impacted my dating life as well (at least those ones that were worth mentioning).

There should be no reservations about asking for help. It's fundamental in relationship building.

It was more than people wanting to help. I actually needed the extra help and support. My strength felt like it was on a rollercoaster where on some days, life felt easy and I could manage. On others, I felt entirely weak on so many different levels. I found I was getting tired and worn out from trying to be everything to myself. I had to let go of the ideology that I was able to support myself in every area: physically, mentally, and emotionally. I started to reach out of my comfort zone and started to call on friends for support. Sometimes, this came in the simple form of a conversation. Sometimes, it was sleeping on a friend's couch, and other times, it was just a hug. Although in retrospect, I could have and should have asked more from those around me, I know their support not only helped me, but also helped draw our bonds closer to a much deeper level of understanding and meaning.

In the process of asking for and accepting help, I had to make some fundamental changes.

I allowed myself to be vulnerable

I had to allow myself to be vulnerable which meant I had to be ok with allowing myself to open up and expose myself without fear. Back to the analogy again, it's like standing in front of a mirror naked, completely exposed. I had hidden my life and my pain from so many people for so many years. I had learned to live this double life and now I was breaking the walls down. I was not only exposing myself, but I was then asking for help which was counter to what I had built up for so many years. I allowed myself to be shot down, but the reality is that is not usually what happened. I found that my friends and my family wanted to help and that drew us closer.

I stopped always playing Wonder Woman

I'd like to think of myself as very capable and independent, but I had to admit in certain areas, I couldn't do it all. I'll be honest, when I came to the realization that my life was so far off track that it was unrecognizable, that alone took some of the wind out of my sail. It's like waking up one day and realizing that everything you had been working towards and the entire direction of your life was off track. It's a humbling experience, to say the least. So as excited as I was about getting everything back on track, I couldn't carry the weight of the world on my shoulders. I needed to stop pretending I was Wonder Woman.

I actually experienced some sort of phenomenon when I committed to resetting my life. Although I felt strong and healthy, I was going through so much healing and learning that I quite frankly didn't have the energy and the capacity to do what I might have been able to do otherwise. I even had struggles for the first couple of months going to the gym. I honestly needed the help, as it was this intense repair my body was going through. It was like shedding my scales as a snake or becoming a butterfly. I was changing and I just couldn't focus on everything-- I really needed to focus on my transformation. Even after I got out of this repair mode, I still couldn't always be Wonder Woman. I needed to hang up my costly costume and only bring it out for Halloween.

It was the same as my father and doing plumbing-- why not leave it to the professional? My dad *could* figure out how to get it done, or he *could* go get his license, but why?! Why should he spend the time, money and the frustration where there is a professional that is trained and skilled in that area?

Or rather, I needed to treat my own life like I do at work. When I hire staff at work, I find people that exhibit skills that I don't have and, as a team, we complement each other because we all have different strengths that we bring to the table. With all that in mind, leverage the people around you. Many people around you want to help you and there is nothing wrong with that.

I gave myself permission to be loved

People usually give because they want to. It's done out of a good place in their heart and might even be a part of their love language (some people show affection by doing for others and rejecting that can actually be hurtful to them).

My staff at work was a great example of those who show their affection through the act of doing. Every year, the staff would get together and plan the birthdays for everyone on the team. I try to forget I'm getting older, but they always reminded me when my birthday was coming up a couple of months in advance. I'm not one to show off or make a big deal of my birthday, but they absolutely loved planning and got enjoyment out of the surprise and the presentation. They were so thoughtful in everything they did: the decorations, the dessert(s), and the gifts -- everything was well thought out. It was their way of showing they cared and they got more joy out of it than anyone! Although, I'd rather fly under the radar, I had to accept that this was their love language and I came to terms with having a desk covered in decorations to celebrate me on my day. It's funny that as much as I didn't want it, I actually came to love it because I felt their love and appreciation, which has since made me love and appreciate my special day that much more. To be completely honest, I think I grew to love it, but we'll keep that our secret! When I finally started to allow myself to be loved, it actually changed the way I viewed my birthday decorations and the birthday in general. It allowed me to see that people were showing their affection towards me, instead of me being hard-headed and stubborn.

I started recognizing the energies of giving and getting

I had no problem giving of myself and my time. I would have gone the extra mile to help people in my life and people knew that, but I hated asking for help. Honestly, I hated to inconvenience people, which is how I viewed help -- someone being inconvenienced on my behalf.

I wanted to tile my closet and my friends had offered to help. Although I was reluctant, I was trying to make an attempt to get over my feelings on accepting help and they came over and spent a Sunday with me. It ended up being far more than we expected and they were going to have to come back to help finish up. I needed to get it finished, but I reverted back to my stubborn self and I went on Craigslist and found someone to finish the job. I found someone that could come with no notice (red-flag #1) and he would tile the closet for $100 (red-flag #2). He said he would be over in a couple of hours (by 5pm) and when he didn't show by 6:30 (red-flag #3), I called him and he said he had fallen asleep (red-flag #4). He arrived a little after 7pm and the whole thing went completely south from there. He decided to cut the tiles in the bathroom and it ended up looking like someone unloaded bottles of baby powder everywhere. It was a mediocre quality job and left a lot to be desired. The next few days, the texts came flooding in from this guy and he ended up having some kind of infatuation and obsession with me, and somehow, his attempt to be flirtatious ended up changing to threatening me with guns. My inability to ask for help from my friends resulted in me going down to the police station and opening a case with the police department because my life had been threatened. So that's what I got for blocking the true desire and energy from my friends that wanted to help! When I finally admitted to my friend what I had done and what transpired, she reminded me of a time I stepped in and helped her without any reservation. She wanted to help and I needed to step back and realize that that's what friends do. I changed the course of the energies by being stubborn. I actually push people away when I don't allow them to help when they truly want to.

I stopped making it all about me

Now, it's not always the case that someone will be able to support you in the way you need (maybe they don't have the financial means, the time, the willpower, etc.) but we should not feel wrong about asking for help (and yes, I still struggle here, even as I'm writing this). For me, I didn't want to inconvenience anyone and I didn't want to put myself out there (being vulnerable) just to get shut down. This is a mentality that we need to get over. Remember what we talked about in the chapter about being vulnerable and letting go? We need to be ok with the outcomes.

If someone does not have the time or the means to help you, that has nothing to do with you. People have other commitments and constraints on their life and if they can help you, they will. There's nothing more and nothing less to that statement. If we make everything about us, then we are setting ourselves up for failure. If it's a no, then it's a no. Move on! There doesn't need to be an emotional connection to the no (let it go). Find another alternative or another route, but there is no sense in getting worked up over someone saying no. It isn't always about you so don't take it personally!

I'm not promoting a message to not do anything for yourself. Just because we don't know how to do something doesn't mean that we have a pass to never learn how to do new things. I mean we have to start somewhere, right? I'm not encouraging you to not try and learn, as we should try to push ourselves and become better-rounded. The point I want you to take from this is that we do not need to be stubborn and try to do it *all* on our own, especially if it is more than we can reasonably take on.

Learning to ask for help has been an incredibly vulnerable experience and I get rather uncomfortable eliciting help. Part of the issue for me stemmed from someone always wanting something in return, but that is not how everyone operates. There is an ebb and flow of life, there are energies that flow, and I could feel that I was inherently disrupting the flow by being adamant about refusing help. I had to let go and let it happen, even if it did make me a little uncomfortable. Sometimes, you need to get uncomfortable to get comfortable.

~~~~~

- You don't have to be Wonder Woman or Superman in every part of your life.
- People want to help you.
- There is a natural flow of energies around asking for help and helping others. Blocking this limits our ability to build connections and relationships with people in our lives.
- You will have less anxiety in your life when you stop trying to do everything yourself.
- It's good to challenge yourself, but be realistic when you need to engage others for help. Could you be doing something more productive and purposeful with your time? If

the answer is yes, then consider asking for help.

Step 4: **Elevate**

You've learned so much about how to RESET your life to this point and now it's time to take it to the next level with Elevate. So many times in life, I wanted to be in control, I wanted to hold on to anger, and I wanted to be validated in my negativity. I came to understand that all these toxic things kept me from moving forward.

Looking back at my own transformation, I was surprised that many of my situations didn't change, but the way I viewed them did. Before my eyes, I changed from a person who used to hold onto anger and resentfulness into an empowered woman with an enriched life. I reframed the most powerful muscle in my body and it was working for me, not against me!

Now it's time for the rubber to meet the road for you too. Let's focus on purpose and living in today.

Chapter 14: Purpose Driven Life

I stood for nothing, so I fell for everything.

I had zero idea of what I wanted out of life, who Jen Sugermeyer was at her core, where I was headed, what made me happy -- I was just moving through life. It's no wonder my dating life was a mess. Why would another human being want to align with someone that is ping-ponging her way through life? I allowed my bosses to dictate my job and career path, I spent my time doing activities that didn't serve me in the long run, I had people in my life that didn't bring me joy and brought me down, and I had literal and figurative 'stuff' collecting dust in the corner that I never used but held on to. Sure, I did a lot of travel and had great experiences, I had some great people in my life, but overall, I did not have a defined purpose for my life.

Purpose is the reason something exists – its aim, goals, satisfaction. Purpose helps to guide your decisions and your direction. I never stopped to determine what this meant, so like a pinball in a pinball machine, I was along for the ride.

When I thought about writing this book, I looked at myself in the mirror one day and said, "Who are you and how did you get here?" It was almost as if I had gone in a time capsule and had come out 15 years later and was trying to figure out what had happened. I don't know how to explain how I got there other than I just did. My life seemed to have a series of twists and turns, people came and went, relationships started and stopped, jobs moved me around, and all of a sudden, there I was in Dallas, Texas, looking at myself and wondering just how I ended up there.

Now, to be clear, even with a purpose, some people's purpose leads them through a series of twists and turns, people can come and go, relationships will start and stop, jobs can move you around, and you may still have a host of questions about your life. We don't really get to choose all the steps our life will take (remember the letting go and giving control to a higher power?), but we do have a choice on how we view our life and our mindset around it. Keeping your purpose in the forefront will help to keep you grounded and on course, no matter what that looks like. Couple that purpose with that mindset and you'll be prepared for anything that comes your way!

I love the saying, "If you have no aim, you will hit your target every time." This is what happened in my life when I blinked and wondered how I got to where I was. I had a few vague goals: do well for myself, advance my career and retire. But none of those had goals tied to them that were quantifiable. They were moving targets.

What did advancing my career mean? Was this advancing by title? Was it in getting money? Was it advancing because of my level of happiness? Remember I never liked the interview question when I was asked where I saw myself in five or ten years? I honestly did not have a straight answer. I had no idea where I saw myself in two years. It was whatever I made up on the fly. I just knew I wanted to retire one day and do well, be financially independent, but no real goals on how I was going to get there.

My life looked like some sort of maze where my path was dictated by unforeseen walls. There's a goal in a maze which is go get to the end, but outside of wanting to retire one day as my end state goal, I was just bouncing around wherever the game took me. My life was directionless. I was tired of this vagabond lifestyle and I knew that my life could have much more meaning if I was actually aiming at a target.

I was often frustrated with my life because I felt like I was floating around with no real direction. I did have some semblance of structure in my life. I got up and worked out, I went to work, and I had friends. I had a life, but even with all of that, I was still floating around feeling as though I did not have a purpose-driven life. I was just living. I think it's important to understand that because I believe that you probably have an element of a schedule you adhere to, kids you might need to tend to, deliverables at work, and people you interact and do social things with -- all of that can still happen, and yet you may still need to define your purpose.

My life was relatively structured and I had a pretty full agenda (minus my incessant drinking after hours -- what a colossal amount of time wasted). What it lacked were the tangible goals. I lived more for pleasure. If I wanted to have dinner with friends, I did it. If I wanted to stay up late, I did it. If I wanted to change jobs, I did it. It was not as if I did not have a full plate, but my decisions were based around which way the wind was blowing, not necessarily because I was striving for anything in particular.

I remember talking with a counselor once and the first thing I told her was how frustrated I was because I felt I was wasting potential. I knew what I had inside of me and I knew I had the capacity to really make an impact in the community, but I never did anything about it. My potential -- I knew I was full of it, I knew I was wasting it, and yet I still allowed much of my life to be dictated by what I wanted to do. I more often than not aimed at a bottle after work and that pretty well dictated how I spent my time—it was purposeless.

As one of the standards I set for myself, I made the decision to engage in purpose-driven activities and seek to find *MY* purpose. This included not just purposeful activities, but also people that served a purpose (which we touched on previously).

Let's first look at the why and then how as we conceptualize the value and meaning of purpose.

Purpose will help you stay focused in life.

Again, if you are aiming at nothing, you will always hit your target. Having a goal will force you to focus on where you are driving to. It's hard to have one without the other. If you are going to have a goal you are actively working towards, you will be focused and driven.

Goals will help you to learn to better commit.

If you want to achieve a goal, then you have already committed to a goal. You may have many obligations and requirements along the way that you will need to commit to in order to achieve your goal.

Having a purpose will give you tangible goal to work towards.

Using my corporate work as an example, since I did not have a purpose or goal for where I wanted to be, I really was not working a tangible program. I was effectively following whatever path my manager carved out for me. I didn't take real ownership in where I wanted to be until later on in my career (and some of this comes with maturity). If my goal is to be the CEO of a company, then I need to develop the path and begin to take the proper steps for execution. Now, I will push back on accepting roles or going in a direction that does not align with my long-term vision for myself.

Purpose gives meaning to life.

When you feel you are working towards an end state, then you've given your life meaning. A life that does not have purpose has no real destination. It helps you to answer who, what, where, when, why and how to end up at your destination.

Goals makes life more exciting!

Have you ever played a video game and you just kept playing until you won? You are so focused on winning, that even when you lose a round, you find yourself just as engaged and a little more motivated than when you started the round the last time. You may have learned something to do or not to do, so you are convinced that this time, you are destined to beat the round! You may spend hours and hours at the game all with one goal in mind -- winning. You could have been sitting on your couch doing nothing but you decided it would be more fun to play a game. Goals make life more fun. Who doesn't like to feel accomplished?

Living for a purpose enables you to have a more intimate relationship with yourself.

You become more aware of your strengths and areas of opportunity. When you set goals for yourself, then you are working with yourself to accomplish what you set out to do. Think about a sports team. It's important to know the other team members' strengths and weaknesses if you want to win the game.   You may win by pure luck, but if you know who is better at defense, who is better at offense, who is strong in scoring, and who is good at moving the ball forward, this will help to define who does what on the field. Your goal is comparable to a sports game, you have to navigate the field and leverage your strengths to win. This will help you better understand those areas where you excel, areas you need extra support, and you'll learn to encourage and support yourself, creating that more intimate bond with yourself.

Purpose keeps you motivated.

You are constantly striving to do your best and get over that finish line! You may come to a path or two that is unfamiliar territory and slows your progress, or you may fail at times, but you keep trying until you get to where you want to be. It's ok to play a level two or three times, but don't we all want to do our best so we can get past it and on to the next level? Setting goals for ourselves creates an innate drive in all of us to want to do our best and finish.

You will attract others that have goals and a purpose for their life.

As we discussed, like attracts like and it's important to be surrounded by like-minded individuals that are also driven (hopefully, you've weeded out the deadweight you've identified in your life already). I remember I went on a date once with someone that came from a lineage of money. I can so vividly remember asking him about his life, how he spent his day, hobbies, etc. His answer was he didn't need to do anything because he had enough money. So, since I was stuck with this guy at a restaurant, I tried to be nice and kept asking questions (if I could have swiped left and been done with him I would have). I asked him what his goals were and I'll never forget his response. He said, "My goal is to get out of bed every morning and not to spend all my money." I mean, I suppose that's a goal, but by no means was that the kind of goals in a man I was looking for. But since I was also lacking some significant goals in my life, this was probably why the two of us ended up eating pizza together that one and only time. I want to attract and be surrounded by people that have purpose in their life.

Clearly, there are lots of very positive benefits to having this level of structure in our lives where we are seeking to accomplish one or many goals. But where do we start? Where do we start when we want to sit down and create a list of what we want to accomplish in life and what goals we want to achieve?

First, think about what drives you and what your interests are.

Maybe you have a passion for children, or the homeless, or a sport, or a certain hobby, or a religious group, or your family, or cooking, or giving back, and so on. Set yourself some goals in these areas, something you would enjoy doing. It might be volunteering or it might just be recommitting time to a hobby, but whatever it is, write down a few things that spark your interest.

What is it that you want out of life?

Where do you see yourself?

Do you have an end-state goal? To get there, what steps do you need to take? Can you break it down in five-year increments? What goals do you need to set in order to get to the end state?

What brings you the most joy?

What people, places or situations make you happy? We should want to do things that bring more happiness into our lives. They say a happy employee will produce better results and naturally give more than what is expected. Same holds true if we are happy. We will produce better results and give more than expected.

What are your strengths?

Knowing what we are good at will help define where we should be focusing our goals. This is not to say that we can't have a goal or learning or mastering new skills, but we should also leverage what we know and what we are good at. I know that I am not very good at basketball (contrary to the popular beliefs of anyone that has ever seen me). If I diligently practiced, yes, I might improve some, but guaranteed I would never make it to a women's basketball team. I actually have no desire to do so. It doesn't bring me joy and I find it rather frustrating. So I don't think becoming a woman's basketball champion is going to make it to the list.

Now that we have the why and the what, start to detail your how. How are you going to accomplish the goals you set out for yourself? Don't make a list of too many goals. Start with a few and walk through how you plan on accomplishing them. They could be short-term or long-term goals, but at least start driving towards something in your life. Attract those like-minded individuals and start to elevate all areas of your life.

Let these be your standards and if something does not serve those areas, then that is your boundary. Find your purpose and give your life the direction and the why. Why are you on this earth? Hit your target and get out of being that vagabond. Make a bullseye out of this game called life!

~~~~

- Purpose eliminates the ping-pong effect. If you're aimlessly driving around in your life, then you are living life like a ping pong, bouncing around.
- Purpose helps guide you in life and gives you goals to achieve. It gives you a reason for doing things.
- Life becomes more enjoyable when you work towards something.
- Purpose brings happiness, it's the meaning for existence.

- Living for a purpose will help you attract others living for a purpose.

Chapter 15: Make Gratitude your Attitude

Gratitude is another one of those buzz words you hear but what does it really mean? We already went over positive thinking and every principle we talk about overlaps. They are all interconnected. Since your objective here is to reset to get maximum results in the areas of health, wealth and love, it's important to talk about all angles so you fully grasp the big picture at stake.

Positive thinking is taking a situation and putting a positive spin on it. Positive energy is the spirited force you emit, and gratitude is the practice of being appreciative and thankful for what is in your life. The practice of gratitude will result in positive thinking and emitting positive energy, but positive thinking and positive energy do not always result in the practice of gratitude. Therefore, understanding the fundamentals of gratitude will, by default, aid in other principles as we discussed.

Gratitude can be displayed in a variety of forms. You can show your appreciation through emotions, actions, or feelings, but however the form, it is fundamentally feeling thankful for what you have (people, places, things, experiences, etc.). This may come naturally or it may be a concerted effort on your part to take a step back and appreciate everything you have. Just as with all the other principles we've discussed, the more you practice, the more it becomes who you are.

I remember shopping for my first car with my mother when I was 16. We went to a dealership and told the sales guy my price point. He disappeared and drove a car from the back with the tag '911' hung around the rearview mirror as its unique identifier. I remember thinking how appropriate 911 was for this sad vehicle, as it probably just came from a police impound lot! Needless to say, this car and I did not have a love affair at first sight! To date, it is still my favorite of the cars I've had, as it ended up being such a huge source of happiness for me, despite all its flaws. I remember breaking the windshield wipers when I tried to launch the snow off my windshield and they never worked the same way again (they would stay on for days at a time even when there was no rain). I remember when the tubing came loose around the sunroof and I ended up soaked one morning, after a midnight rain, as I was driving out of my driveway to go to work. I remember when the window stopped working and I had to throw money into the toll-booths through the sunroof and missing most of the time. All of these little nuances only made me love this car even more. It was like this special friendship this car and I had. I was a poor teenager working in a dry cleaner trying to pay back my parents for this 911 vehicle. Although it wasn't perfect, it was so loyal and I was grateful to be able to get around without hitch hiking (yes, I've put my thumb up for a ride many times), walking, or even taking the bus. I didn't focus on the silly imperfections. I was grateful and loved this vehicle for getting me from point A to point B.

Why is it important to live in gratitude? Outside of making you a more positive thinker and able to naturally generate more positive energy, studies have shown that there are many positive impacts to being thankful for the things in our lives.

People who live in gratitude are generally happier and more fulfilled in life.
When you look at all aspects in your life and give thanks for what you have, you will start to feel that what you have is enough. Please don't misunderstand that this means you'll never want any more. It's not wrong to want more. Gratitude just means that you appreciate what you have and if this is all you ever had, you would be happy and fulfilled. It doesn't mean that you don't strive for more or have desires for other things. Minimizing your life will help you to see what you have around you and appreciate the things that serve a purpose in your life.

Gratitude gives you stronger relationships.
You start to look at friendships and interactions on a deeper level and appreciate the conversations, traits, and attributes of people in a way you may have overlooked. This makes you generally more engaged with the world. You are able to build stronger relationships since you are focused on finding the good in people. Additionally, gratitude makes you naturally emit a positive energy which attracts other positive vibes, so you are now surrounded by uplifting and positive relationships in your life.

Gratitude gives us the "feel good" in our lives.
You are not just acknowledging a situation to be positive, you're eliciting a feeling/emotion when you are truly thankful.

Gratitude helps us to favorably deal with differences.
Instead of focusing on the differences, we focus on what is positive, albeit from similarities or differences. More people will start to gravitate towards you because they like the energy and vibe you give when they are around you. You make them feel wanted, you acknowledge them as a human being. Your appreciation for who they are is complimentary. Who doesn't want to be around someone that compliments them? We want to be around someone that appreciates our humor, our banter, our style, our quirks, for both our strengths and our weaknesses.

Gratitude reduces envy
You should not be focused on what others have, but focus on what you do have. Do not envy others for their life, but be thankful for what you have been blessed with.

Gratitude gives us a more optimistic outlook on life
Knowing that whatever comes your way will be something you should be thankful for gives you a more positive and optimistic outlook. It gives you a way of looking at things in your life holistically.

Gratitude helps improve self-esteem
You can appreciate the small things about you that make you unique and the things you do well. I have the blessing of being 6'1" and although it didn't seem like a blessing when I was 14, it has become my favorite quality about myself. I am grateful I can reach the top shelf, I am grateful I can change a lightbulb without a ladder, I am grateful my head is above the crowd at a concert, and I'm grateful that I'm always able to see above a crowd! I have learned to appreciate the benefits of my height and I can truly say I am grateful for how I was

built! We need to appreciate who we are, what we can do, our characteristics and our strengths, and let go of everything else. As a result, your self-esteem will improve.

Gratitude helps to put what you do have into perspective. Much in the same way as I described my self-esteem, gratitude will help you realize just how good you have it! If you are always focused on what you do not have, then you have completely overlooked what you do have. They say money cannot buy happiness. Why is that? Because you need more than a pile of money to make you happy. If you did nothing but sleep on that money, I can't imagine that alone would be able to give you a level of happiness.

Now money may afford you opportunities you might not have otherwise, but there are plenty of people that have money and no happiness. On the flipside, there are plenty of people that do not have money and are entirely content. How can this be? Shouldn't money make you happy? Absolutely not. People that are happy have been able to find the good in their lives and remain focused on that, regardless of their bank account. These people have a perspective of life where even if they have a rough day, they can still manage to come home and love on their animal, embrace their family, give an unwarranted compliment, and genuinely keep a smile on their face because they know there is more in life than just the rough day. It's letting go of those situations that do not bring us joy or add purpose, letting them roll off the shoulders. For the record, we just tied together self-esteem and letting go with gratitude. Are you now starting to see how gratitude is a fundamental building block for your life? Maybe those seemed easy to connect, but what about minimalism? How would minimalism overlap with gratitude?

Believe it or not, gratitude is harder or impossible to fully achieve if your life is not minimized.

We talked about minimalism as an important part of being able to identify what has importance in your life. It keeps clutter and distractions out of the picture. It simplifies our lives which allows us to focus on not just ourselves but to also think about what is truly important. Unfortunately, we live in a sensory overloaded society where we are constantly bombarded by stimulation and material objects. When we allow too much stimuli in our lives, we actually are not able to fully appreciate what we do have. Materialism reduces the ability to focus on what we do have, since we are overwhelmed with options and are often vying for more. Therefore, once we boil our lives down to what is truly important and ridding ourselves of excess, we can have a better overall appreciation for what we do have.

Have you ever had a meal that included so many ingredients you couldn't taste some of them? You may have seen on the menu what the dish included, but some elements were so overpowered and got lost in the overall composition of the dish. On the flip side, have you ever had a dish that was simple and only included a few ingredients? Think about the appreciation you had for each ingredient as you savored the dish. It is the same concept if you have too much in your life and something is getting overlooked, muddled, or underappreciated for what value it does bring. Simplifying your life will help you appreciate all the facets you have both material and immaterial.

In my own life, I knew that I had a lot to be thankful for, but I never was. I was stuck in a mentality where I felt like everything happened *to* me. I had to stop feeling like a victim that didn't have enough and change the way I looked at the blessings in my life. I even learned to be grateful for the challenges by looking at them as learning experiences which were allowing me to even further enrich my life.

Small changes in the way I viewed my situation helped me to recreate an entirely different outcome. I focused on what I could be grateful for and what lessons I could take from what was happening. I had to let go of my ideology of what should have happened, and instead, accepted the outcome for what it was and found reasons to be thankful for why it happened.

- **I was laid off from my job.**

  - **Without gratitude:** I was angry. I couldn't believe I had dedicated my life to a job, moved states for this job, and then I was let go all because we got new executive leadership in my department. I viewed this company as my family and just like that, I was terminated? I was left high and dry when I pushed 60-80 hours a week when the company was struggling for staff, put blood, sweat and tears into the company, and they left me to struggle? What loyalty was that?

- - I was a victim

- o **With gratitude:** As the new executive leadership had taken over, I quickly found that I was not entirely aligned with the direction of the company. I had become rather discontent and I had started looking for other opportunities outside of the company. Being let go forced me to find a situation where I was better suited and helped me in my career growth.
    - - My life was enriched

- **I was divorced by the time I was 30.**

  - o **Without gratitude:** I was bitter that I had made such a huge mistake. I now had a blip on my life resume that I couldn't undo. I was going to have to admit to any potential suitors that I had already been married and it was a status on every form I'd have to fill out. I'll never just be SINGLE, I'll always be DIVORCED. Will I be treated as damaged goods or will men wonder what is so wrong with me and shy away from me because of my past? I had wasted 6 years of my life and now I had to start completely over. What about children now I am that much further behind from the idea of kids becoming a reality? That was really a mistake.

- I was a victim

  o **With gratitude:** There were aspects of the marriage that worked and others that didn't. I now had the opportunity to take a step back and assess what I truly wanted out of a relationship. Admittedly, I had dived into the relationship very quickly and I myself didn't have much of a foundation to stand on. I was not whole as a person and I realized that I just wasn't ready. I began to appreciate the situation for what it could teach me and how I could get stronger from it.
    - My life was enriched

- **My family was more well off than I was.**

  o **Without gratitude:** I was constantly harboring ill feelings that I was not able to do things as comfortably as they could. I was the only single income and it was hard to make ends meet. Why did it feel like gifts were always an expectation? I'm already drowning! Why did I feel like I could never get out from under the financial barrier I was under?
    - I was a victim

  o **With gratitude:** Someone told me one time that he wished he could give his mom a gift. She had passed away several years previously and he missed the ritual. I was grateful I still had my parents and I needed to take advantage of the times I do have. I also didn't have to give a gift that required money and I had to be ok with that. I also acknowledged that my life was rich in so many other ways. I had so many experiences, I had friends of all walks of life, I was fulfilled by giving back to the community, I had so many friends, and I had support everywhere I turned. My life was a very colorful pallet and I was painting a masterpiece. I really did have a good life regardless of how much money I had in the bank. I was rich!

- My life was enriched

- **I was passed over for a promotion.**

  - **Without gratitude:** I couldn't believe I had not even so much as been given an opportunity to be interviewed for the internal position I applied for. The company instead, brought in someone off the street! Couldn't they have had even the decency to give me the opportunity to interview and tell them about all the things I had done in my past? How did they know what I was truly capable of? I bet they didn't even look at my resume! I had worked so hard to make my resume looked good and I even got the support of my boss to go for the position. What a slap in the face to see someone sitting in the office, and not only that, but this person became my new boss! What a shock and how rude, after being with a company for several years.

    - I was a victim

- **With gratitude:** I realized quickly that the position I wanted involved much more than I realized. Although I could have done some of the job well, I was not positioned well to take on the full scope of the job description at that time in my career. I would have been trying to climb a ladder without proper footing and it could have ended disastrously. Instead, I got to learn from my new leader and filled in the gaps from my own skill set.
  - My life was enriched

You see, there are two very distinct ways of looking at situations. Looking at life with glasses of gratitude helps shift the perspective entirely. I first experienced every one of those situations without gratitude and I had to change the way I viewed them. I was able to help eliminate the anger and harbored feelings. Then I looked at how the very same situations actually are valuable additions to my life. It helped to take a weight off me and I was much more happy and content in my life.

When I decided to make gratitude my attitude, I became grateful for the little things, which actually made me put less emphasis on the big things. I began to appreciate all of the ingredients in the recipe that made up my life. Another beautiful outcome of being thankful for everything in my life was I was more appreciative of myself and all my life ingredients!

~~~

- Gratitude helps shift your perspective to appreciate what you have, which will help you find the good in everything.

- You can find gratitude in not just seemingly 'happy' situations, but also in challenges, life lessons and trials. Be grateful for *everything*.
- Focus more on teachable moments and learn from them.
- Rather than harbor anger against people, become thankful for the lesson they brought to you.
- Remember, you are no longer a victim, so re-shift your mind to find what you can learn from a situation and find gratitude in it. From victim to victorious!
- You will feel free when you look around and are thankful for what is in your life.
- Gratitude in all areas of your life is true maturity, and the power is in your mind. You can do it!

Chapter 16: Living in Today

There are three distinct timeframes in our lives: past, present and future. I found that living in the past only weighed me down and stunted my growth. Living in the future kept me from appreciating the present and living in today gave me freedom over my life. Commit to putting boundaries in place so you can live in the present and live in that elevated state of being.

Living in the past

The older we get, the more 'stuff' we have to reflect on. It's good to have memories, but it's not good to let any negative memories hold us back from moving forward.

After I made the decision to stop drinking, I was faced with a lot of pain to weed through in order to rid myself of the past that held me back. I had to realize that none of these situations defined me as a person, nor could I continue to allow them to be a crutch for me to hide behind. I was always too afraid of dating someone that had their act together because I knew I had areas I needed to work on myself. I knew I needed to stop drinking all together and once I did, the victim mentality needed to stop. I needed to acknowledge just how much I truly brought to the table and my value in a relationship. I needed to stop shying away from men that had good jobs and didn't suffer from the same addictive behaviors that I did, but instead tell myself I was allowed to have a higher standard. I was not defined by my past, I was not flawed, and I was not broken. Nothing was unforgivable and I had to come to grips with the fact that all of it lived in the past. But, until I could really acknowledge that the past was the past, I was stuck believing I was defined by it.

What I found was holding on to the wrongs in my life was like being a prisoner in my own skin. Even prisoners can be exonerated which is exactly what we need to do in our own lives.

Living in the future

It's good to set goals. We talked about the benefit they have when looking at living a purpose-driven life. Again, if you aim at nothing, you will always hit your target. Therefore, aim ahead and make sure you are setting yourself on the right track for the older you. But setting goals for yourself for the future and letting the unknown dictate your actions are entirely two separate tracks of thinking about the future.

I had a friend share with me once that she lived with a fear that dictated what moves she made in the present. On the outside, my dear friend was always anxious and worried. There were always a thousand reasons she could give for why she felt she had to worry. She had a lot of dependencies on her and she didn't want to fail. She was concerned about the future for herself and for her family, and wanted to be a great mother, I am sure a lot of people can relate to the fear that comes with just being a parent wanting the best for their children.

What I missed from my friend was the smile, the laughter, and the ability to just enjoy life in the moment because there was always something in the back of her mind that kept her from achieving happiness. She was constantly in fear. As I listened to her talk about her concerns, I believe that all of them were valid concerns, but the problem was she had concerns for anything and everything outside of her control. What if this happens, what if that happens, what if nothing happens, what if everything happens? It was like looking at a playbook for a football team, but instead of focusing on what her team was doing, she was worried about the one player on the other team she didn't account for, coming in and stealing the ball. Instead of feeling confident that the play she had put together would work out, she was worried about that one player on the other team who kept her distracted from remaining focused on the game at play.

Sometimes, we are so focused on all the 'what-ifs' that we forget to enjoy the fact we made it to the NFL, are playing in sold-out stadium, and are able to provide for ourselves and our family today because of the opportunity of being chosen to be on the team. We are blinded from seeing the cheering fans supporting us, the cardboard signs people made with our names on them, showing their love and support, and from reveling in the fact that we are playing with some of the most talented players in the industry. Instead, we are fearful of not doing well, not winning the game, losing the ball, throwing a ball that gets intercepted, tripping, or not making a touchdown. Could you imagine being in this situation where you have accomplished so much that you made it to the NFL and you never got to enjoy it because you surrounded yourself with 'what-ifs' and let fear block your enjoyment of today?

There's no coach that will have a locker room talk with the players after the game and tell them the players on the other side did 100% of what was forecasted. There are just too many variables. We don't know what the other coach advised as a defense strategy and still, it's up to the players to execute. The players may have their own idea of a defense strategy which introduces a ton of unknowns into the game. However the game plays out, both teams made it to the end with a chance of either team losing! The point is the goal is to finish the game and do your best (and probably to win), but if you really think about it, everyone was a winner because they were alive after the game. They hopefully had fun along the way and made it to the end of the game.

Everyone knows the odds of winning and losing-- one team will win and one team will lose. Therefore, you might as well enjoy the game for what it is. If we are paralyzed in fear because of the idea of losing, then we are bound to miss all the amazing moments along the way. But are you really ever losing? Because maybe, just maybe, we need to reassess our goal of winning to include goals like enjoyment, having fun, happiness and other pleasure-based goals.

There are so many of us out there that are letting the "what ifs" of the future stop us from seeing our fans, enjoying playing on green grass, and appreciating the game for what it was intended for -- enjoyment.

Living for today

After taking a step back on my life, I finally learned to live in the moment. I learned to appreciate what was in front of me and what I was dealing with at that exact moment. I didn't want to keep reflecting on and replaying the past. I didn't want to live in fear of the future. I wanted to be happy right where I was.

So how do we change this mentality when we have been held down by our past and our future?

Gratitude

We talked about the importance of gratitude and how it influences how we view what we have. If it's small or large, we look at everything with rose-colored glasses and find the beauty or the purpose in what we have. This appreciation will help you to better live in the moment, since you are focused on the good that is right in front of your face.

Ease up on yourself

So often we put so much pressure on ourselves in regards to what's coming up in the future. We get so concerned with what we want to happen that the stress keeps us from being present today. I learned to loosen up on myself and focus on how I could not be so serious with myself all the time. Don't be too hard on yourself and learn to ease up a little. When you make it to the NFL it's an accomplishment. If you win, it's a bonus. Make sure you are able to enjoy the moment and not get stuck because you are too hard on yourself.

Take ownership of your life

As I've mentioned before, I played the victim too often in life. I blamed situations or others for the way things turned out, even the state of my emotions. But in the end, you have to take responsibility for the things that are truly your responsibility. So, I decided to take ownership of my path today. I didn't allow anyone else to dictate my direction because I know that it's being guided by my higher power.

Forgive

I had to learn to forgive people, situations and myself for mistakes of the past. I had to clean out the blockage in the plumbing and create peace with my past. There were people I had to contact to make amends to clear the guilt from my conscience. Especially as it comes to making peace with yourself, you need to do an inventory of your past and acknowledge what is holding you back and what you keep reliving, and forgive yourself. Accept that it was your past and let go.

Stop Worrying

I had to stop fretting about the future and trying to control things that I had no real control over. I had to trust that I was making good moves, that they were being guided through my meditation time, that I could course correct along the way, and that being connected to my higher power would help me find the right direction. My favorite verse of the bible (so much so I tattooed it on my body) is Jeremiah 29:11:

> *For I know the plans I have for you. Thoughts of peace and not of evil to give you a future and a hope.*

I know the intent for me is to have peace in my life and a good future, so I choose to believe that my higher power sees much more than I can see and is helping to guide me to take the necessary steps in the right direction. Some of these steps may be challenges to help me better understand my strengths and weaknesses, and they may not feel like blessings at the moment they happen. Some of these steps may be character development opportunities. Some of these steps may seem like failures to help strengthen me for the future. I don't know why many things happen, but I do believe that someone is driving the ship and I quite frankly don't want it to be me anymore. I let the worry go to my higher power, and what a relief that was.

If you are constantly worrying, then you are not focused on your today -- you're stuck in the weight of your past or the fear of the future. Live and let live. If you want to experience an elevated life then you need to be focused on the here and the now. Be present and it will help you appreciate what is around you.

~~~~

- Living in the past keeps you from moving forward.
- You are not defined by your past.
- Living in the future creates worry and anxiety about the things that you can't control. Anxiety can lead to chronic health problems.
- Living in the present makes you more content in life. You are able to appreciate life's little moments.
- Pay attention to your senses; sight, hearing, smell, taste and touch. Find the joy in all of them and appreciate the color and delight they bring to your life!
- Don't take life too seriously.
- Learn to laugh at situations and all throughout life.

~~~~~

Elevate is a critical part of RESET because focusing on being present and living for a purpose will help tie all the prior principles together. The concepts in elevate help you achieve maximum benefit out of life. When your mind is in the right space and you are purposeful about what you are willing to accept in your space, then you start to live the life you envisioned you'd have. Your newfound perspective will give you happiness which will resonate throughout your life. You stop muddling through, living the rinse and repeat life and begin to look forward to your days. You can then apply what you have learned to your life and discover what truly brings you happiness, purpose, and your highest priorities in life.

Although my life appeared to have structure from the outside, I was dancing on the edge of a high-rise, one step away from disaster. I was living in hell and I had little to no power over my life and the direction it was taking. I knew my life outside of the office was in utter disarray and I was out of energy from keeping my two worlds apart. As much as I thought I had two distinct lives, the truth was they bled into each other. I woke up in fear every day, thinking about what had happened the night before. I was constantly on the defense at work, going above and beyond, trying to compensate for the utter train wreck my life was elsewhere. I was anxious and fearful at all times. I couldn't sleep, I always had a million thoughts racing through my mind, and my heartbeat was constantly racing. If I didn't have a complete breakdown in life, I was a key candidate for a heart attack.

Then came those seven words, "You need to learn to love yourself." I was in the midst of World War III and all it took was a soldier to say, "Hey, all it takes to win is you!" What I learned through this journey, and mostly from failed attempts for over a decade, was that getting a hold of my life was more than just starting or stopping a behavior. I had to crack open every part of me and face it in the mirror. I had to look at my thoughts, my actions, the people, places and things in my life, what made me happy, what made me sad, what standards were acceptable, what boundaries needed to be established. I had to learn to say no, I had to learn to speak up, I had to learn to be vulnerable, I had to learn to forgive and start with myself.

The soldier was right, it was all about me. Through all the various areas I addressed and the improvements I made, I saw my life start to change. I was now at peace, my anxiety was better managed, my sleep was regular, my friendships were stronger, my relationship with my job improved, I was a better employee, I had purposeful and enriching activities, the relationship with my family improved, and best of all, I actually did learn to love myself.

My RESET took me to a place I never had been, but always knew I was capable of. I erased my old way of thinking and I strengthened my mind to bring me to where I am today. My world continues to evolve and for once, I am excited for the future. I no longer welcome the turbulence on a plane in hopes for a crash. I know just how much I have to live for and I love my life.

I want nothing more than for you to experience the same level of joy and satisfaction I have in my life in all areas, especially in the areas of health, wealth and love. You will find that your life will start to blossom across all areas of your life if you follow this methodology and in the order of this book. What you'll also start to find is that a lot of those things that fell between 'low hanging fruit' and toxic that you weren't necessarily a fan of you may actually learn to appreciate. I found appreciation in my job, people in my surroundings and even in traffic after going through this program. You are reframing your mind so allow the process to work in your life and let it evolve. Don't fight it, just work it.

It's completely attainable to have the life you want and to love the person in the mirror again-- there is nothing in your life that is preventing you from achieving it other than you. It's all about understanding how these pieces interconnect and looking at your success holistically. You are the key to unlocking your own success.

Celebrate you! You made it! I am personally so proud that you are where you are at. I can tell you, my life today gets better and better as the days pass. I told someone that I am untouchable and I mean it. There is nothing anyone can say that is going to impact me or throw me too far off-guard. I have made my mind into a machine and I am not only untouchable, but I'm unstoppable. I'm optimistic about life and for the first time I am able to let people see inside and experience all of me. I have no more demons in my closet, no hidden life, nothing I get embarrassed to share. I removed the power from anything that was keeping me held captive (not just my addictions, but the shame of my past) and I am finally free. I want you to have what I have and it's entirely feasible. This was an incredible journey and I am so blessed to have scrapped my knees so hard that I had to go through it. I don't believe that I could confidently say this statement had I not gone what I went through, but I love myself. I love everything about me and RESET showed me the way.

Step 5: **Transform**

You have now walked through the fundamentals of a transformational RESET, but to be truly transformed, you need to equip yourself with the tools to maintain it. It's like high school. I took a lot of subjects, but I forgot most of the fun facts I learned because I never revisited them. This needs to be a lifestyle, not just a book you read, take some action, and then forget. If you want change to stick, you need to transform your life once and for all.

I can tell you from my own experience that every time I made progress in my life, if I didn't pick up a drink for a day or two, I thought I was on the road to a full recovery. I was always greeted with a nasty reality when I picked up that drink again and my progress turned into lost hope that I actually made a permanent change in my life. I was always treating the symptom and not the true problem. In order for me to fully address the problem, I needed to create a lifestyle that would support everything I learned during my one-year journey. I want to share with you how I finally transformed my life once and for all, making this a truly holistic and sticky program with long-term results.

Maintaining a Lifestyle

If you've actively participated in this book, you've likely done some soul searching and self-reflecting. Whatever led you to read this book, it's in your hands to complete your own reset or enhance you life. It may be an addiction, depression, some past trauma or abuse, a lifestyle, overworking, an eating disorder, a mentality, a loss of identity, shame, fear, or anything that has the power to hold you back from optimizing your life. The good news is there is hope for you. Shackles can be broken and I want the peace and freedom for you that you deserve.

But I also can't want it more than you. You must take the responsibility. You have to call the last of the Day 1s. You need to say, "Enough is enough." You have to commit and follow the steps I've outlined in this book.

As with embarking on any journey like this, know that you will stumble. There will be struggles along the way, challenges that crop up that you weren't expecting, emotional turmoil and people who won't support you. During those times remember that your only job is to learn to love yourself just like I did, and honestly, nothing else matters.

Recognize, Eliminate, Structure and Elevate gave you the tools and resources to set your foundation, take power over your mind, and establish the necessary boundaries for your success. Now we are going to address how to take what you've learned and transform those into a lifestyle and maintain it to best position you for continued success. Reading and applying it to your life are two distinct steps in the process because reading this book might give you knowledge but knowledge is only knowledge until it's applied. Then it becomes a skill we can use forever in our lives.

Making the concepts in this book habitual is where you will see growth in your life. This section focuses on maintenance like tune-ups for your car. These are tips and tricks to help keep you on track to make sure your vehicle stays in alignment. Without checks and balances, you run the risk of slipping back into your old way of life which you've already committed to leaving in the past.

Steadfast -- you got this!

It's a lifestyle!

People often ask me what diet I follow. My answer is always "I don't diet, I have a lifestyle." Yes, there is a method to my eating habits but my eating isn't a diet, it's how I eat every day. I set a standard for what is acceptable and my boundaries dictate what I eat. It's a lifestyle, not a diet. I don't think about what I'm going to eat, it's premeditated. Almost everything I eat has been thought out in advance. I've spent years studying health and calories, I've done body building competitions, I've done the fad diets, and I finally found what works for me. I eat cake (or just the frosting), I eat chocolate, I eat ice cream, and I pretty much eat whatever else I want.

How?

Lifestyle. Simple as that. I probably spend 85% of my time eating very routine and standard meal: protein and vegetables. Since I have my routine meals already planned (down to the portion size), I know in advance what I'll be eating and how many calories I'll be consuming. It makes the mathematical equation simple. I know how many extra calories I can eat on non-standard food.

I could go on about the methodology behind my eating, but what I want you to take from this is the lifestyle approach that I have to my eating. Again, I have people asking me all the time what I eat and most people are shocked when they see me eat the vat of frosting, but I have it all planned out, so I can.

If you are looking for a change in your life, you need to look at this change as a lifestyle. You see, for me, a diet is daunting. It makes it seem like we are depriving ourselves of something. I stay pretty fit and I don't feel deprived at all. I'm happy with my protein and vegetables. I know that's my lifestyle. Small meals every few hours is what I do. Then, someone has a birthday, and bam, I'm eating a cupcake like a boss! If I was on a diet, then I would look at those cupcakes and be sad because I would want one. For years, I tried to quit drinking and failed. I looked at what everyone else had and I wanted it. Now I say my lifestyle is alcohol-free and I don't miss it, nor do I look at others with envy. I have made it known to my family and friends that this is now who I am and no one presses me to do otherwise.

You may have something other than drinking or dieting that you're resetting, but whatever you are going through, embrace it as your new life. Don't hold on to the old you or the old ideology and romanticize it. Let it go. Those habits and beliefs helped build you into the person you are today, so be grateful for that, then let it go and move on. Put those boundaries in place and stay in your lane!

Revisit the principles- not just a one-and-done

You've committed to adopting your new mindset and outlook as a lifestyle, now you need to commit to revisit the principles you've learned. It's clear from the daily list of To-Dos that I made in the beginning of the book that life has a lot to balance and moving pieces. There are constant distractions that can keep us preoccupied. With all those moving pieces, it's imperative we revisit what we've learned so we don't forget.

Think about math class in high school. Do you think you could list all the formulas you learned? I was a math wiz and I know I struggled when I went to take a prep course for the exam to get into grad school-- I had forgotten almost everything!

I don't want you to forget what you've learned here. You will not see a lifetime of benefit if you read and forget. I want you to get the very most out of life, to experience the joy you deserve. I want you to be able to use the tools and mindset in this book to navigate through life and bob-and-weave as punches come your way. Not just this year, but for the rest of your life. This is exactly how I coach my clients to keep on path.

Think about revisiting the principles as you would a warranty. If you get a warranty on a ring you bought at a jeweler, they will want you to come in every six months so they can clean, tighten, and ensure the ring is in top shape. Otherwise, the ring can become dull from the daily exposure to the elements. It can loosen and you are at risk of losing the diamond/gem, or you could diminish the quality of the ring if it becomes beat up and scratched. Taking it in for a cleaning will ensure your diamond is secured tightly, all of the muck will be removed from the band and the stones, and the ring will sparkle as you leave the store.

Going through this book once and wishing your life would change won't be fruitful. To really get the full benefit and to keep shining like a diamond, you need to keep going back so your warranty stays up-to-date.

Have you ever read a book or watched a movie and you picked up on something you didn't read or see the first time? It's the same thing with our lives. Your view on the world and your life is going to continue to evolve, so when you go back and review the topics in this book then you are very likely to pick up on new things. It not only keeps us shiny, but you will see things differently as well as you will pick up on ideas and concepts you didn't think about previously.

Self-reflect constantly

We should be aware of ourselves at all times. Think about your life like you would when you're driving a car. You need to constantly be aware of your speed, the drivers in front of you, behind you and beside you. You are headed to a destination and you need to be aware of the exits to take as well as the speed, you have to time yourself so you arrive on-time, and so on. If someone veers into your lane, you may need to pump the breaks or move. Being aware and alert will help you navigate your journey successfully.

As it applies to your life, you should constantly be reflecting on what is happening in your life, what is going well, and what could be improved upon. There will be situations that veer into your lane and you need to be prepared to navigate them. You may or may not have handled the situation as you should have, and either way, you should think through the situation and assess how it went.

There is nothing selfish about thinking about yourself. If you don't, who will? You are responsible for your destiny, so being in tune with your thoughts and actions is key.

A CEO once asked me about the single thing I do that contributes to my success. I said "self-reflection". It has given me a better understanding of who I am and what I stand for. I have a higher degree of emotional intelligence and it challenges me to constantly be improving upon myself.

Don't be afraid to think about yourself. In fact, I encourage you not to just date yourself, but self-reflect as often as you can. It's a key to your success.

Learn to say NO

I want you to say NO. Right now, I want to hear it. Shout "NO!"

Get used to saying that because you're going to be saying it a lot more as you start to set up boundaries. If you tend to be a people pleaser and you're used to saying YES, you need to forego this mentality and put yourself first.

It's quite liberating, actually. It gives you back the power over your life. Two simple letters can communicate such a strong message. If someone asks you to do something you don't want to, say NO. That tells them where you stand on an issue. That's power.

You teach people how to treat you by what you are willing to accept. People will not intuitively know unless you tell them, done both verbally and non-verbally.

I mentioned in an earlier chapter that I was willing to give all my time, sanity and even zip code to company. Since I was working around the clock, what I communicated was that I was ok with the amount of work I was doing and they gave me exactly what I was willing to accept. I watched people around me that had families and relationships that would go home at the end not stressed and crazed, yet I was constantly in a state of frenzy. I have no one to blame other than myself. It wasn't the company that made me crazy, it was what I was willing to accept. Had I said no, had I left with my coworker, had I left my work at work, then I would have had a much better quality of life. I needed to say NO.

If you do not communicate when a boundary is being pushed, then you run the risk of your boundary being crossed. It's as simple as that.

It's not just telling others NO, it's also telling yourself so that you get to say YES to you in the end.

Those boundaries are the framework in which you are willing to operate. If you are being tempted to go outside that wall, then you need to stop yourself.

Take it easy on yourself- just aim to be better today than you were yesterday!

I don't know that even Mother Teresa did life perfectly. I don't know anyone who has. We need to have realistic expectations and not be too hard on ourselves when we feel we fall short of where we want to be or in the timeframe we expect it.

We often want to accomplish our goal and move on. But this is life we're talking about not a literal puzzle where the last piece means we've finished. This is life and it's evolving, it changes day-to-day, and we are in a constant state of movement. There really is no 'end state' as long as you are sucking air. All you can do is try to better yourself and aim to be better today than you were yesterday. Simple enough.

Let's say we live until we're 85 years old. That's 31,025 days on this earth. Can you imagine doing anything perfectly 31,025 times? That would be one heck of a record. Honestly, who is to say there is a 'perfect' way to live? As long as we are aiming to be our best selves, we are self-reflecting and trying to improve from our lessons learned, and as long as we are aiming to be happy, trying to be good people, then we're really not doing too badly for ourselves!

Aim to be better today than you were yesterday and ease up on yourself if you fall short in an area. Think about where you could have done better and be better tomorrow.

Moderation- build your foundation first

Moderation -- the single most hated word in my vocabulary! I don't think I'm the only addict that despises that word (if addicts could conceptualize that, then there wouldn't be addiction now, would there?). It's a concept I struggle with in all areas of my life. I overdo everything!

I actually find my inability for moderation in my behavior a little frustrating, but I suppose it can be beneficial as well. I'm sure my job has greatly benefitted from my 'all-in' work ethic.

On par for the norm, I went to go buy a bicycle once -- first one in my adult life. I went into the bike shop and bought everything I would need to ride: the bike, chaffing butter, the squishy shorts so you don't hurt your lady-bits, a cup holder, blinking lights for the night time, a bike jacket, a bike vest, and a really expensive seat. Literally, I walked out of the store looking like a cyclist (quite literally because I changed before I left so I could go on a ride). I was all-in for about 4 rides and there ended my biking career. I probably could have just bought the bike. That would have been moderation. Being overly passionate can be a good thing, but it can also bring on a lot of anxiety (and wasted time and money).

As part of my transformation, I committed to working on moderation, trying to be less overly passionate about just anything, and be a little more strategic with my time and energy. I'm not saying you shouldn't be intense or have passion. In fact, I want you to be intense about committing, reprogramming and resetting your life. Still, I want you to take moderate steps. If you try to turn all the knobs at the same time then it's going to feel overwhelming. If you take on too much then it will feel like it's too much. You won't be able to fully appreciate all the principles in this book if you are working on all of them at the same time. Once you've been able to process and understand the fundamentals, then I hope you are full steam ahead.

I want nothing more for you than for you to take yourself and your life seriously and live with intention, but you will hinder your progress if you take it all on at the same time. When I made the commitment to change, I followed my heart and did what it told me to do. All the while, even though it was contrary to my personality, I knew that each step I took, I needed to process and conceptualize.

This will be key to your success moving forward. It's a crawl, walk, run kind of journey. Be intense about what you're doing but do it in steps. Once you are running, then go all out and embrace the life you have now built for yourself, but don't sabotage your foundation where it will fall on you if you don't build it properly.

Walk through each chapter as they are listed and move on when you are ready.

Be aware of what you consume

Most of my friends know I'm one of the more eclectic individuals of the circle and I'll try anything just about once. If it's a concert, show, sporting event, or anything that sounds fun, there's a good chance that I'll give it a go. Since I have a very diverse personality, there's no saying where I'll end up.

One of my best friend's in Dallas and I love to frequent metal and rock concerts. I love a good heavy metal show. It can really give me a pep of energy! I have found, however, that I do need to limit the amount of metal I listen to because of how amped I can get when I listen to it. I'm not bashing on the genre, it's my response to the music that I need to pay attention to. I need to find the balance of music that puts me in a more neutral state so I have that balance in my life.

I've found that when I'm consuming an excess of anything

heavy or aggressive in nature where I find myself with inflated energy, then I need to do it in moderation. I've found that anything in excess that is too heavy in nature will weigh on me and I may even find myself in a more negative state. I'm not suggesting to cut out healthy, heavy activities, but make sure you are cognizant of the amount you are consuming. Without your awareness, you may be pumping the wrong kind of energy or messages into your life and it can derail your course.

In my own life, I can see the difference in my mindset by the music I listen to. I find myself wanting to drive faster or more aggressively when there is an intense song playing. Just be mindful of what you are consuming so it doesn't have an adverse effect on what you are trying to accomplish.

Look at your past as building blocks and reflect

I believed I was defined by my past. I couldn't have healthy dating relationships because I felt unworthy because of what had happened in my life up to that point. I didn't think people would understand my past, so I kept my life hidden. I was ashamed and embarrassed at everything in my life up to that point and the shame lingered with me. To free myself, I needed to change the way I viewed the past and look at my past as a series of building blocks that built the person I am today.

Take what you've learned in your life, reflect, and learn from every situation whether good, bad or neutral. When I'm in my time of meditation, I think about what I could do better that day than I did yesterday. Even in your best state, you should be seeking ways to improve yourself tomorrow. What went well today? What could be improved? What shouldn't be repeated? Set your intentions for what you want to work to improve. Aim to be better every day (minus the beating yourself up), and the building blocks will help raise you up.

It took a long time to conceptualize. It's hard to sever the thought that all these horrific things in your life are not who you are, but they really are not. Life is a series of twists and turns, changes, and learning experiences. I had to set my life apart from who I am and know that even in some of the darkest times, some of the most shameful experiences, some of the times I would rather forget -- all of those helped make me who I am today. Without that past, I would not be writing this book and hopefully making an impact in your life for the better. I became a confident, strong, compassionate advocate for life and myself, all gifted to me because of the scars that gave me wings. You are not defined by your past.

It's OK just to be OK

If you've looked on social media, it's easy to believe that everyone has a picture-perfect life. No one posts on the dysfunction or what people don't want you to see. People post rainbows and kitty cats, vacations and happiness. We're led to believe that people have these beautiful lives, peaceful, happy, successful, and rarely will you see the other side of the coin. It gives the impression that our lives always need to look like they do on Instagram and Facebook. In case you hadn't figured it out, that's not reality!

My life did not look like Instagram or Facebook. My life was not OK. Even in the throes of my internal battles, I still managed to post pictures portraying happiness. It's usually a façade. Everyone does it (I'll tell you now that I believe my social media matches my life!).

Regardless of what social media shows, it's OK just to be OK. Everyone is only showing what you want to see, not the full picture. No one is sleeping on a bed of roses. That's not reality.

I had to be OK with just where I was at, which was often in the midst of a struggle. I had to get honest with myself and be comfortable with awkward feelings, the changes, and not feeling like a smiley face. It was especially helpful and refreshing to be forthcoming with people in my life so they could understand what I was going through. If people only see smiles and happy photos, how will they ever know what you're going through?

When I was going through these especially rough times, I had to set my eyes on getting to a better place, and work to get there. You may be dealing with grieving the loss of someone, a missed opportunity, a diagnosis from the doctor, but whatever it may be that is weighing on you, work through the steps you've learned, to improve the situation in your mind and move forward.

It's OK just to be OK, but it's not OK to stay there.

Honestly- we need to talk about honesty again?!

Honesty is so key, so we're going to talk about it again. We're taught as kids to be honest. How many of us were punished for telling a lie or hiding something? Why? Because we were trying to cover up the truth. Same is true for your life. You need to be honest with yourself: what's going well, where you're at, where you're struggling. If you lie, you're only harming yourself by covering up and not addressing the truth. Smothering the truth doesn't make it go away, it just buries it and festers inside of you, or manifests itself into something unintended. We discussed this in the beginning, but I don't want you to forget that you will stunt your growth if you do.

It's like when I told myself I was ready to start dating. I knew my drinking needed to be addressed before I ventured into any kind of healthy relationship with another person. Instead, I lied to myself and to everyone I've ever dated that I was ready and capable of a relationship. Needless to say, they all failed. I actually thought I could hide my drinking in some of the relationships and even those crashed and burned. Until I got honest with myself and improved my own deficiencies, I was only adding tally marks to the number of failed relationships I had.

Communication is one of the key elements to any relationship. Regardless of the depth of the connection, if we know what the other person is going through, then we are able to help rationalize the situation in our minds. Think about someone that you work with that had a change in their productivity at work. Maybe you started to think negatively about this person because it appeared they no longer cared about their job. You were having to pick up some of the workload and you could see the business was impacted from this behavioral change. Then one day, you found out that your coworker was at his wife's funeral. What you didn't know was that your coworker was dealing with a wife that was undergoing chemo and it impacted his performance at work. Now your perception about your coworker had completely changed. You now had a level of sympathy that you didn't have before. In fact, you voluntarily took on additional responsibilities above and beyond what you were already doing just because you knew it would help him out and you wanted to help make everything more comfortable as he grieved the loss of his wife. Think about how much better this situation may have been if you understood upfront there were heavy personal issues happening. Not everyone is going to be able to open up and talk about their issues. Some people are more reserved and quiet by nature, so maybe you need to just ask in a very nice and caring way. Had you asked to buy him coffee and just see how things were going, maybe this would have created an avenue for your coworker to feel comfortable to tell you what was going on. I'm going to suggest to you to be honest with the people around you. It doesn't mean you need to go spew your business to everyone, but there are some people that could probably benefit from knowing where you are at and what you are going through. It will benefit you as well.

You've committed to being honest with yourself and with others in your life. You don't have to post your feelings and your struggles on social media, but you do need to address them. If you let them fester, all you're doing is harming yourself and stunting that growth.

Talk back to yourself

I am giving you full permission to talk back to yourself. You need to keep yourself in check sometimes. If you don't, who will? Your mind got you into this situation in the first place, so if it starts getting off course, tell it where it needs to be!

I'm an addict, so I have addictive tendencies for most everything. This means I pretty much can overdo anything, even the most benign things you could think of. My brain is constantly looking for something to give it happiness, so it gravitates to things that pleasure the reward system. This becomes an issue when I lose control of moderation, especially if the 'thing' can cause harm to my body. I find myself going on autopilot and all of a sudden, I'm drinking 12 cups of coffee a day, or consuming a Costco size bottle of cinnamon a week, or using a bottle of spray butter a day, or drinking multiple bottles of wine every night, or you name it. I have the capacity to overdo just about anything. These all just happened, I didn't conscientiously look at any of those things and think to myself that I should create a dependency. It just happened. Much in the same way as a parent will tell their child no, I now have to tell myself no. I have to be aware of my weaknesses and outsmart them. I have to be my own voice of reason.

In the event your brain is telling you YES, you need to tell yourself NO to whatever prevents you from being where you want to be. It goes along Freud's Id, Ego and Super Ego theory, where we have an aggressive side (Id), a moral side (super ego), and a realistic mediator between the two (the ego). You have to become the voice of the ego and talk reason into your situation if you find your Id is on the loose.

When our Id starts to get off track, we need to tell it to stop. There is absolutely no shame in having an outright conversation with yourself. Think of it like a little pep talk. I suggest you even talk to yourself out loud. I find these to be more impactful and I don't get sidetracked as easily.

Point is, don't be embarrassed to talk to yourself. It doesn't mean you have multiple voices in your head, it means that you are holding yourself accountable and in tune with your actions, providing real-time coaching like I would with you in person if you were a client.

Keep your mind open

Your mind is the key to your success, it's you most powerful source of strength. As you go through life from here on out, your mind needs to be open to change. Otherwise, either nothing is going to change or you'll be fighting an uphill battle, never to arrive at your target destination.

Remember Blockbuster, the physical store that rented movies? They were adamant about keeping movie rentals only in their physical stores even though technology was advancing and the Internet was becoming more prevalent. Their inability to adapt to customer demand ended up being their demise, and their competition swooped in and offered an on-line option for consumption. Blockbuster ended up going out of business because they were unwilling to keep an open mind about the changing times. There will be circumstances in your life, inside and outside of your control which will cause the need for change in your life. You don't want to end up like Blockbuster because you were unwilling to adapt.

Wherever you are at in your life, you have to keep an open mind because the world does not sit still. There's a saying that if you're not moving forward, then you're moving backwards. The world is constantly moving and I'm not just saying that metaphorically. We are literally rotating on an axis. Don't let the world pass you by because you're not willing to open your mind and accept the changes.

It's funny what a baby can do to a family. I met a woman with a fairly conservative husband who was not overly accepting when his daughter got pregnant out of wedlock. The entire pregnancy, the husband had some pretty high walls and was adamant about his position. She sent me a picture the day their grandson came into the world and my eyes immediately filled with tears. She said, "We just welcomed the birth of our grandson and he's already working on his grand pappy's heart." This man was looking at his grandson with such admiration and it was clear those walls were breaking down. This man's life will be forever enriched because of the bond he was willing to make. He course-corrected his mindset and ended up with the love and joy of a little baby boy.

Like it or not, we are getting older every day and things are happening to our bodies. We can choose to fight it, but at the end of the day, our faces are still going to sag, more hair will come out of our noses, our ears are going to get bigger, our hair may change color or fall out, and our metabolism is going to slow down. Change is a natural part of life. You can choose to get on board with it, or you can fight it. The more you fight it, the more you are going to have to keep up with the fight to preserve it (thinking about coloring your gray hair? It's going to keep coming back). I'm not telling you to let anything into your life, but I am telling you that changes happen. It's life. If you aren't assessing how you can fit these changes into your life, then you'll be fighting those wrinkles for the rest of your life.

Open your mind to change, before change happens and you get left behind.

Keep trigger words in your pocket

Keep trigger words in your pocket and pull them out any time you start to veer off track. This is going to require you to have a level of cognizance when it's happening, so pay attention to your thoughts and behaviors. If you start to get angry, to think negatively, if you start to put out negative vibes, if you want to revert back to some old behavior, you need to stop them before they start. Being aware of when you are at the on-set of a change will give you the power to get your thoughts back on track.

I mentioned that my trigger word was my best friend's baby. It was something that put me at peace with the world and made me genuinely happy. Think of a person, place or thing that makes you happy, and commit to saying it when you start slipping.

Here's how it works.

When you identify that you are acting or about to act counter to whatever it may be that you are working on, this is when you pull out your positive word. Let's say you are working on your anger. When your blood pressure starts to rise or you let out one of those really heavy sighs, then I want you to reach in your pocket and pull out your word. Say it on repeat until you've diffused the situation.

Let's say your word is 'palm tree'. At the point your blood pressure rises, say 'palm tree' over and over. Think about why they make you happy, why you chose that word, think about where you've seen one, think about your dream vacation when you first saw a palm tree. Your goal in this exercise is to distract yourself and put your mind in a positive state. Now that you've elevated yourself from the situation. Walk away from it and change your course.

Easy enough!

It's ok to talk out loud as we discussed. Do whatever it takes!

Fight with Love, not Hate

The gentleman that helped me realize I was off track in all areas of my life could have very well ignored me, deleted me, blocked me, or given me a stern talking to. In fact, I was prepared for all of these responses. What he did, however, was sit down with me and it communicated to me he cared about me as a person which helped me to realize that I was worth fighting for. It's easy to get upset, lose our cool and get frustrated, but approaching a situation with care and compassion is going to yield better results. Our relationship didn't last more than another week or two, but his presence in my life was truly a gift from my higher power. Fight for yourself and for others in a kind and compassionate manner-- it's the only reason I'm here today.

Celebrate Y-O-U!

Take joy in where you are at today! There isn't a day that

goes by that I am not truly grateful where I am at and all I've been able to accomplish! Life is to be enjoyed, so enjoy where you are at today! Even if you aren't where you want to be, that's ok. Life is a constant journey, and we should always be striving for 'something'. Everyone dies, but not everyone lives. Make sure you are living life and celebrating you (even when you say, "I'm not OK", celebrate those moments too!).

Final Thoughts

Starting this journey, I decided to take an entire year to focus on myself while I hit reset on my life. I had decades of unraveling to do and substantial reframing of my mind to complete and I felt a year was a reasonable amount of time to get back on track. I started to see some immediate results and within 6 months I saw a drastic difference throughout all areas of my life. After a year, it was nothing short of a 180 my life had undergone. I had accomplished resetting my mind and my direction, and for the first time, I can truly say that I loved myself. What I realized was I was embarking on a life journey and it was going to be forever evolving. Much in the way my life had taken twists and turns to get me where I was, life will always have these challenges. It's about being prepared to deal with them as they arise.

My mind had been overtaken by an addiction that almost killed me, I was suicidal, and I had no self-love or self-worth. I am no longer willing to be a victim in my own body, I committed to taking back control, and by having the right foundation, mindset and boundaries in place, I reclaimed and now maintain the life I deserve.

Regardless of your circumstances, you have to make yourself a priority. It's the only way to learn to love yourself too. What I learned was if I am not at my best, then I cannot give my best. If I neglect myself, then it is not only to my detriment, but to others: my job, my family, my friends, my life.

RESET is a holistic, lifestyle program that is designed to work into your busy schedule. I managed to change my entire life without taking a day off work or neglecting any of my priorities. There are no in-person meetings to attend, you don't have to even leave the comfort of your home. What you do need to do is make sure you are committed and working the program. Be selfish about getting yourself back on track (you may also need to revisit this book many times over or get more personalized help like my clients have). You are more effective to others when you are at your personal best.

I doubt the man that told me I needed to learn to love myself knew the breadth of the gift he gave me, or if he prepared those seven words to have such an effect. I don't think he could have predicted the impact it would have on me or where it would lead me. He was simply someone who cared and he handed me the key to unlock my potential so I seized the opportunity. I wouldn't change a day of my past. It made me who I am today and I don't think I would have truly understood what it meant to love myself had my life unfolded differently.

Achieving the change you want in your life is possible. I'm an example that life can veer off track, but it's never so far gone that you should consider giving up on yourself. Working the steps in this book and continuously reworking them has helped me reset my life and learn to love the person within.

Wherever you are, whatever crossroads you're at, no matter how many Day 1s you've promised yourself, there's no better day to start than today. Get rid of the last hoorahs and the excuses. It's time to uncover the life you deserve and let your scars be your wings too. Congratulations, it's time for your RESET and to celebrate you!

About the Author

Jen Sugermeyer was inspired to create and write "RESET" to help those struggling to find themselves and live the life they truly desire. Her trademarked process is based on her own personal experience leading a double life, worried that her two worlds would collide. Through her book and programs, Jen hopes to give others what took her so long to figure out -- how to love the person looking back in the mirror.

Jen's life appeared picturesque on the outside. She was a successful woman in corporate America, physically fit, owned a house, gorgeous truck, traveled the globe and had stories for days. Behind the smile, she had many deep-seated internal struggles she kept hidden for decades. Jen's double life almost claimed her life until seven words changed her thinking and she was finally able to break the cycle of destruction and find lasting change. After reclaiming power over her life and her mind, Jen finally found happiness, purpose and love. Now, known for her concept of "dating yourself", her mission is to help those who have lost their self-love and identity along life's journey.

Jen is a lover of life and now she can earnestly say of herself as well. Learning self-love was the key that unlocked her potential and helped her find her purpose. She loves impacting the lives of others and strives to get her message out to help transform as many people as she can reach.

When she isn't writing or coaching, you'll find Jen and her 6'1" self boxing (watch out, she's a southpaw with a reach!), exercising, being both in front of and behind the camera, traveling, spending time at the lake, hanging out with friends, family, and doting over her niece, Olive.

Originally a Virginia native, Jen is now a Texan who lives with her cat, Booger, in the great city of Dallas. For the last 15 years, Jen has worked in corporations around the globe in Washington, DC, Afghanistan, Virginia, California, Texas and even spent a couple years in Italy.